2015

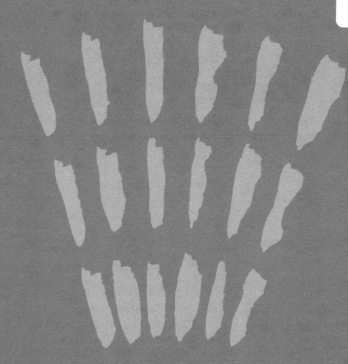

Latin America and the Caribbean
in the World Economy

The regional trade crisis: assessment
and outlook

UNITED NATIONS

Alicia Bárcena
Executive Secretary

Antonio Prado
Deputy Executive Secretary

Mario Cimoli
Officer in Charge, International Trade and Integration Division

Ricardo Pérez
Chief, Publications and Web Services Division

Latin America and the Caribbean in the World Economy is the annual report prepared by the Division of International Trade and Integration of ECLAC. The ECLAC subregional headquarters in Mexico and the Division of Production, Productivity and Management assisted with the preparation of this year's edition.

The production of the report was overseen by Mario Cimoli, Officer in Charge of the Division of International Trade and Integration. Keiji Inoue, Senior Economic Affairs Officer with that Division, was responsible for its technical coordination. The following staff members of the Commission assisted in the preparation and drafting of the chapters: José Elías Durán, Sebastián Herreros, Nanno Mulder and Dayna Zaclicever of the Division of International Trade and Integration, and Wilson Peres and Gabriel Porcile of the Division of Production, Productivity and Management.

The authors are grateful for inputs provided by Sebastián Castresana, Daniel Cracau, Tania García-Millán, Mario Saeteros, Jorge Mario Martínez, Javier Meneses, Laura Palacios, Andrea Pellandra, Gastón Rigollet and Roberto Urmeneta.

Explanatory notes:
- Three dots (...) indicate that data are not available or are not separately reported.
- A dash (-) indicates that the amount is nil or negligible.
- A full stop (.) is used to indicate decimals.
- The word "dollars" refers to United States dollars, unless otherwise specified.
- A slash (/) between years e.g. 2013/2014 indicates a 12-month period falling between the two years.
- Individual figures and percentages in tables may not always add up to the corresponding total because of rounding.

United Nations publication
ISBN: 978-92-1-121901-2 (print)
ISBN: 978-92-1-057230-9 (pdf)
ISBN: 978-92-1-358018-9 (ePub)
Sales No: E.15.II.G.5
LC/G.2650-P
Copyright © United Nations, 2015
All rights reserved
Printed at United Nations, Santiago
S.15-01141

Contents

Introduction

With external conditions sluggish and highly uncertain as the global economy still struggles to shake off the effects of the economic crisis of 2008-2009, the Latin American and Caribbean region is not isolated from these effects and is projected to record a small drop in gross domestic product (GDP) in 2015, followed by a weak recovery in 2016. Against this backdrop, 2015 will be the third consecutive year of increasing declines in regional export values; a state of affairs not seen since the Great Depression of the 1930s. This poor performance reflects the end of the commodity price boom, the slowdown of the Chinese economy, the weak recovery of the eurozone and the lacklustre economic activity in the region, particularly in South America.

The sharp slowdown in world trade following the crisis is due largely to the persistent weakness of global aggregate demand, which the industrialized countries' expansionary monetary policies have failed to galvanize. Several elements contribute to this scenario, such as a global excess capacity in several industries, the instability caused by the disconnect between financial and real-sector activity, high levels of public debt in the largest economies, sharply deteriorating income distribution in many countries and the slowing of the Chinese economy. The intensive process of production fragmentation that had been boosting global trade since the 1980s has also come to maturity. The new conditions could well shorten regional and global value chains and, therefore, further deflate trade.

Trade and investment relations with China have also had a major impact on the region, particularly in South America. Despite strong growth of trade flows with China up to 2013, bilateral trade relations suffer from several problems. The region's trade deficit is widening, with exports concentrated in a few countries, products and companies and consisting basically of raw materials. Foreign direct investment (FDI) flows from China are still small and, because they benefit extractive activities almost exclusively, they entrench the inter-industrial trade pattern. The region must therefore take advantage of the changes under way in China to diversify its exports towards higher-value-added and knowledge-intensive products and services. In the short term, there are opportunities in the processed food and tourism sectors. Likewise, the interest shown by the Government of China and Chinese companies in investing in infrastructure could be tapped to help close the region's large gap in that area.

The region has made notable progress in implementing the trade facilitation agenda and must make much more. Further advances in this area would boost the low levels of intraregional trade and encourage the internationalization of smaller companies, most of which do not yet export. In turn, this could drive export diversification and reduce the region's heavy dependency on natural resources, especially in South America. More robust trade facilitation could help strengthen weak intraregional production linkages and expand the region's limited participation in global value chains. Lastly, several key principles underlying the trade facilitation agenda —such as government transparency and the promotion of public-private dialogue— are vital to increase the efficiency of the State and combat corruption.

In short, Latin America and the Caribbean is facing the bleakest international economic outlook since 2009. The entrenching of its natural resource specialization during the price supercycle and its persistently low-tech production structure are making it hard for the region to find a way out of the current complex conditions. Although some traction could be gained from the nominal depreciation of several countries' currencies in recent months, it is limited by the narrowness of the export basket. The region must, therefore, deepen its economic integration. Progressing towards an integrated space with common rules is vital to promote production linkages, strengthen intraregional trade and support production and export diversification. Despite the shrinking fiscal space, the region must make bolder strides in designing and implementing industrial and technology policies in order to diversify and increase productivity. Such policies are the only mechanism capable of galvanizing long-term growth, which is essential for creating jobs and reducing inequality.

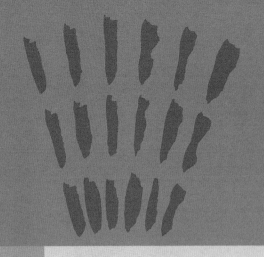

Summary

A. Slow growth and global uncertainty exacerbate the region's weaknesses

B. Opportunities to diversify trade and strengthen linkages with China

C. Latin America and the Caribbean needs to move forward with the trade facilitation agenda

A. Slow growth and global uncertainty exacerbate the region's weaknesses

Exports from Latin America and the Caribbean will decline for the third year running in 2015, with their value projected to fall by 14%. Such a situation has not been seen in 83 years, since the Great Depression, when the value exported fell by an annual average of 23% between 1931 and 1933. The prices of the regional export basket in 2015 are expected to fall more sharply in 2015 than during the last world economic crisis in 2009, with a more marked drop seen only in 1931 and 1933 (see figure 1). Given the inauspicious outlook for 2016, the probability of a further contraction in exports is high.

A fall in export values for three consecutive years has not been seen since the Great Depression

Figure 1
Latin America and the Caribbean: variations in exports by value, price and volume, 1931-2015 [a]
(Percentages)

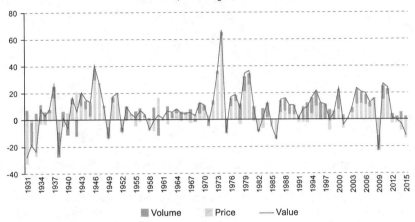

Source: Economic Commission for Latin America and the Caribbean (ECLAC), on the basis of ECLAC, "América Latina: relación de precios de intercambio", Cuadernos Estadísticos de la CEPAL, No. 1, Santiago, 1976; and data from regional indices with a 2010 baseline.
[a] Figures for 2015 are projections.

The recessionary bias of the current international economic context is preventing trade from recovering the dynamism seen before the crisis of 2008 and 2009. Furthermore, changes in the structure and characteristics of world trade are also having an adverse impact. The combination of these factors has aggravated the weaknesses of the region's production and trade structure (see diagram 1).

The weakness of the global recovery since the crisis has resulted from a combination of real and financial variables, together with imbalances in the international economy. In particular, international finance decoupled yet further from the real economy in this period. In the years leading up to the crisis, external financial assets grew much more quickly than gross domestic product (GDP), gross fixed capital formation and goods and services exports, and the gap widened after the crisis. The decoupling of financial products has compounded the imbalances originating in the real economy. Furthermore, the ability of global financial markets to mobilize and leverage resources makes it extremely difficult for governments to prevent bubbles, control speculation in currencies and commodities and limit the non-bank borrowing and shadow banking systems that elude or operate outside of prudential rules.

The macroeconomic policies applied by the world's largest economies in response to the crisis of 2008 and 2009 prevented the crisis from becoming even deeper or more protracted. However, as fiscal space diminished (because public debt increased as a share of GDP or because of the political problems involved in raising expenditure), the predominant course of action became an expansionary monetary policy in the form of quantitative easing, adopted first by the United States and Japan and more recently by the European Union. Although the interest rates in these economies have remained very low for an extended period, inflation has not risen and aggregate demand has not picked up significantly, which confirms the pattern of abundant liquidity and little effective demand.

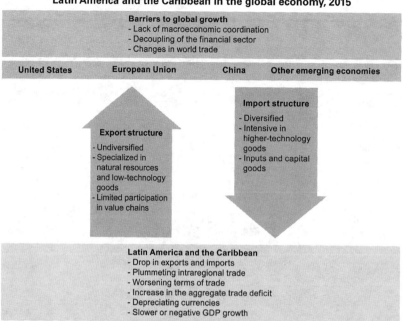

Diagram 1
Latin America and the Caribbean in the global economy, 2015

Barriers to global growth
- Lack of macroeconomic coordination
- Decoupling of the financial sector
- Changes in world trade

United States   **European Union**   **China**   **Other emerging economies**

Import structure
- Diversified
- Intensive in higher-technology goods
- Inputs and capital goods

Export structure
- Undiversified
- Specialized in natural resources and low-technology goods
- Limited participation in value chains

Latin America and the Caribbean
- Drop in exports and imports
- Plummeting intraregional trade
- Worsening terms of trade
- Increase in the aggregate trade deficit
- Depreciating currencies
- Slower or negative GDP growth

Source: Economic Commission for Latin America and the Caribbean (ECLAC).

Another factor that is affecting the global economy and trade is the fact that the exports of emerging economies have slowed sharply or fallen since 2011, even though the currencies of several of these countries have depreciated. This has happened mainly in countries specializing exporting commodities. China's export growth has also slowed because of lower prices and lower demand from its trading partners. The economic model followed by China for over three decades shows signs of running its course, and the growth rate has slowed since 2012. The United States Federal Reserve has been paying attention to this weakness in most emerging countries and other developing countries, expressing its concern about the effects that normalization of its interest rate might have on them.

The persistent weakness of aggregate demand in the European Union has had a strong impact on world trade, since the region accounts for a third of world imports, if trade between European Union member States is included. The shortfall has not been made up by emerging economies such as China, India and Brazil, whose overall share of world imports is just 14%.

Another factor that is negatively affecting trade flows is that Chinese exporters are gradually replacing imported inputs with locally produced ones. They have been able to do this thanks to a long process of capacity-building and scaling-up within global value chains, which has allowed them to gradually reduce the imported content of their exports, especially with respect to high-technology goods. The world trade impact of import substitution in China's high-technology industry has been magnified by the growth in the share of these products in imports to the European Union, Japan and the United States from China.

The weakness of aggregate demand in Latin America and the Caribbean and in several of its main extraregional markets largely accounts for its poor export performance in 2015. Depressed global demand has dragged down commodity prices significantly, especially for oil, coal, copper, iron, zinc, silver, nickel, gold, soybean, corn, cotton, sugar, coffee and fish products. This situation has hit the region hard because it has a commodity-intensive export structure and offers only a limited range of higher-technology products, whose prices have fallen less.

The countries that export oil and its derivatives, natural gas and metals (mostly South American economies) have experienced the greatest drop in exports values and deterioration in their terms of trade. By contrast, most Central American and Caribbean economies (with the exception of Trinidad and Tobago), as net importers of fuels and food, recorded an improvement in their terms of trade. Mexico's terms of trade deteriorated by less than the regional average because, despite being affected by the sharp fall in oil prices, most of its exports are manufactured goods.

In the first half of 2015, the value of intraregional trade contracted by almost 20%. The largest declines occurred in South America, whereas, by contrast, trade between Central American countries increased slightly. Trade between the economies of the Caribbean Community (CARICOM) also fell substantially (see figure 2). The weakness of intraregional trade is worrying because such trade is typically more intensive in high value added products than extraregional trade and characterized by a greater presence of small and medium-sized enterprises (SMEs), which leads to job creation.

Intraregional trade contracted sharply in the first half of 2015, but not as sharply as during the global economic crisis

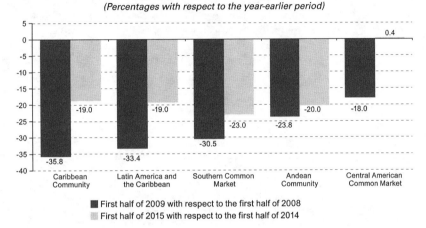

Figure 2
Latin America and the Caribbean (selected groupings): variations in intraregional exports, first half of 2009 and first half of 2015
(Percentages with respect to the year-earlier period)

■ First half of 2009 with respect to the first half of 2008
▨ First half of 2015 with respect to the first half of 2014

Source: Economic Commission for Latin America and the Caribbean (ECLAC), on the basis of official data.

The current situation shows that the region has not added enough value to its natural resource exports, whether by processing them to a higher level, incorporating technological advances with a view to diversifying them or generating new service exports associated with sectors such as mining, agriculture and forestry. This situation reveals a major industrial policy deficit here that must be corrected, since the incentive structure during the high commodity price period did not foster substantial investment in this area by the business sector.

Despite the difficulties of implementing significant industrial policies in contexts of slow growth, the development of new sectors with the capacity to export is needed more than ever. In a crisis like the present one, strengthening industrial and technological policies in order to diversify, raise productivity and incorporate knowledge into production is not only an economic imperative but a mainstay of employment and social stability.

Exiting today's difficult conditions calls for renewed efforts to deepen regional economic integration. Moving towards an integrated regional space with common rules is indispensable as a way of promoting production linkages, enhancing the resilience of intraregional trade and fostering production and export diversification. Consequently, steps must be taken to explore areas of convergence and synergies between integration mechanisms.

B. Opportunities to diversify trade and strengthen linkages with China

China is shifting its economic model away from investment and exports towards a lower-growth, but more sustainable, version based on consumption and services. The economic policy changes under way will be reinforced by the country's next five-year plan, from 2016 to 2020. This model aimed at "building a moderately prosperous society", as the Government of China describes it, envisages slower growth (averaging 5.9% per year over this period). Like other processes under way, including rapid urbanization, it will contribute to shaping China's economic relations with Latin America and the Caribbean in the coming years. The region should prepare to seize the opportunities and address the challenges arising from these shifts in the world's second largest economy.

Latin American and Caribbean trade with China increased substantially during the past decade, when China became the largest driver of the global economy. This trade came with growing asymmetries: a mounting deficit for the region, the concentration of its exports in a small number of primary products and just a few companies, inter-industrial trade flows with limited linkages with global value chains, and a large share of environmentally sensitive products in the region's exports. Unless suitable policies are put in place to contain them, these asymmetries will most likely grow in the coming years.

Growth in the region's exports to China has occurred mainly in crude or processed natural resources. Imports of medium- and high-tech manufactures from China expanded more rapidly than exports, generating an increasingly negative trade balance for Latin America and the Caribbean (see figure 3). The value of exports to China has fallen since 2014, owing chiefly to lower prices for the main export products, while imports from China continue to expand.

Figure 3
Latin America and the Caribbean: trade balances with China by technology intensity,
2000, 2007, 2010 and 2014
(Billions of dollars)

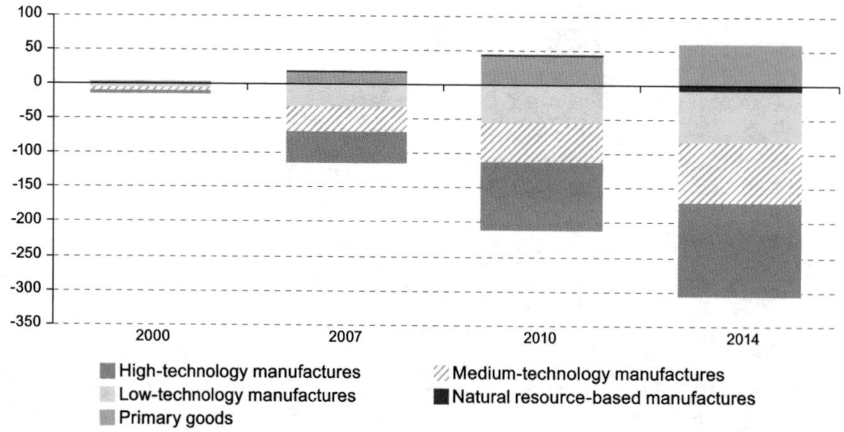

Source: Economic Commission for Latin America and the Caribbean (ECLAC), on the basis of information from the United Nations Commodity Trade Statistics Database (COMTRADE).

The number of products the region exports to China has risen, but remains very low in comparison with its exports to other, traditional destinations. Few firms in Latin American and the Caribbean export to China, although they are increasing in number, especially in Chile, Costa Rica, Ecuador and Mexico (see figure 4). The number of SMEs exporting to China has also risen over the past few years, although they still represent only a small fraction of exports.

Production linkages with China are increasing, but are still weak and concentrated in low-tech products. The countries of the region have increased their share of the foreign value added exported by China, although albeit from very low levels. These linkages occur mainly in mining, medium-low-tech manufacturing and services, especially commerce, transport and storage, R&D and other business services. The bulk of these linkages originate in Brazil, followed by Chile and Mexico (see figure 5).

China has considerably increased its share of the foreign value added embedded in the exports of the Latin American countries. These linkages occur in great measure in medium-high-tech and high-tech products, which reflects the large intermediate goods component in the region's imports from China.

Figure 4
Latin America (9 countries): share of the five leading export firms in total exports to China, 2012
(Percentages)

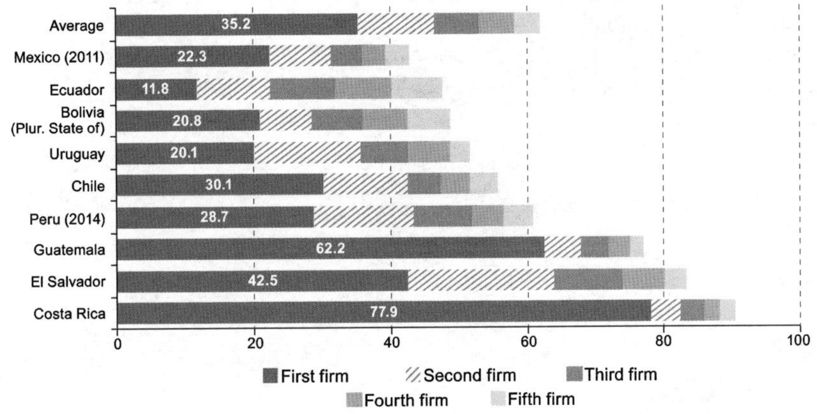

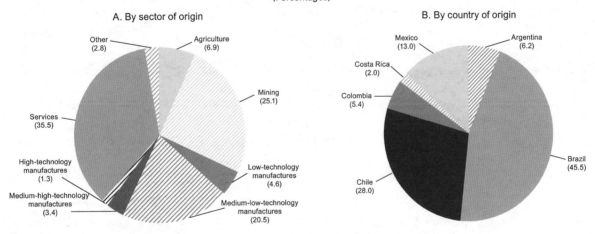

Source: Economic Commission for Latin America and the Caribbean (ECLAC), on the basis of microdata from the customs services of the respective countries.

Figure 5
Latin America (6 countries): structure of value added embedded in exports to China,
by sector and country of origin, 2011
(Percentages)

A. By sector of origin

B. By country of origin

Source: Economic Commission for Latin America and the Caribbean (ECLAC), on the basis of Organization for Economic Cooperation and Development (OECD)/ World Trade Organization (WTO), Trade in Value-Added Database (TiVA) [online] http://www.oecd.org/sti/ind/measuringtradeinvalue-addedanoecd-wtojointinitiative.htm.

Because they are highly concentrated in commodities, the region's exports to China have a larger environmental impact than its exports to other destinations, with greater consumption of water resources and higher emissions of greenhouse gases per dollar exported. In its trade with China, the region is a net exporter of water, but a net importer of greenhouse gases embedded in products (see figure 6).

Although the region's exports to China would have to increase by 80% to reach equilibrium in the trade balance, the main challenge lies in diversifying these exports. The experience over the past decade suggests that the incentives generated by high returns on raw material exports has prevented diversification from occurring spontaneously. China's process of scaling of the technology ladder shows that broadening the region's export supply to China (and to the rest of the world) requires policies geared specifically towards building new production capacities that, in turn, will underpin development in new sectors, products and services.

The region has the potential to become a strategic partner for China in the agrifood market, given that China needs to feed 19% of the world's population with only 7% of its farmland and 6% of its water resources. China's food imports from Latin America and the Caribbean could more than double by 2020. Latin American food exports to China have grown rapidly, but are highly concentrated in a few primary products and in a few South American countries. Increasing urbanization and a rapidly expanding middle class in China represent a tremendous opportunity to diversify the export supply towards foods with a higher degree of processing.

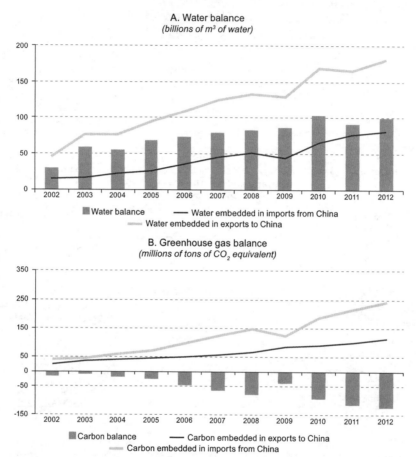

Figure 6
Latin America: water and carbon balance embedded in trade with China, 2002-2012

A. Water balance
(billions of m³ of water)

B. Greenhouse gas balance
(millions of tons of CO$_2$ equivalent)

Source: Economic Commission for Latin America and the Caribbean (ECLAC), on the basis of Rebecca Ray and others, *China in Latin America: Lessons for South-South Cooperation and Sustainable Development*, Boston University, Center for Economic Transformation (CENIT), Tufts University and Universidad del Pacífico, 2015.

In the services sector, tourism is an area with great potential. Chinese tourists are expected to number 100 million in 2015, but Latin America and the Caribbean will receive only 0.3% of this flow. Measures to increase this share would include adopting more flexible visa entry requirements, improving cooperation and air links and offering package holidays suitable for Chinese demand.

Reciprocal flows of foreign direct investment (FDI) also need to be increased. Although China is the second largest source of FDI globally, it accounts for only a small share of FDI in Latin America and the Caribbean compared with the region's traditional investors, the United States and Europe. China's investment in the region is also highly concentrated in extractive industries, especially hydrocarbons and mining. The reforms under way in China could boost the country's outward FDI flows in the next few years. The region should aim to capture a larger share of these flows, by promoting stronger sectoral diversification and linkages with local firms.

Chinese investment could help overcome the region's logistics and transport infrastructure deficits. The limited involvement of Latin America and the Caribbean in global value chains is partly due to high non-tariff trade costs. China's government and businesses appear to be interested in investing in transport infrastructure, which is a high priority sector for the countries of the region. Materialization of such investments would improve connectivity, which would boost intraregional trade and investment flows and attract FDI from the rest of the world.

The Government of China recognizes the strategic importance of its links with Latin America and the Caribbean and is seeking institutional mechanisms for dialogue with the region. Notwithstanding the political and technical complexities, there are shared areas of interest in which common positions can realistically be adopted. This is a task the region must tackle if it wishes to build its bargaining power to negotiate with China in the coming years.

C. Latin America and the Caribbean needs to move forward with the trade facilitation agenda

Trade facilitation has been increasingly to the fore on policy agendas because it offers a way of integrating countries better into world trade. This trend has been reinforced by the development of international production networks (also known as regional or global value chains) and the conclusion of the World Trade Organization (WTO) Trade Facilitation Agreement (TFA) in December 2013. According to WTO, trade facilitation is the "simplification and harmonization of international trade procedures", i.e. "the activities, practices and formalities involved in collecting, presenting, communicating and processing data and other information required for the movement of goods in international trade".[1] The trade facilitation agenda includes five groups of measures: transparency, formalities, institutional arrangements and cooperation, paperless trade, and transit facilitation.

Although the results are better for Latin America and the Caribbean than for other developing regions such as sub-Saharan Africa and South and Central Asia, the region is struggling to reduce non-tariff costs and the time taken by foreign trade operations. Its performance in this area is poorer than that of the developed countries and those of East and South-East Asia. The region's transport infrastructure deficit and inefficient administrative procedures translate into high non-tariff costs for trade, especially in the Caribbean. In addition, for the three subregions of Latin America and the Caribbean, the cost of trade with the United States is lower than the cost of intrasubregional trade (see figure 7). This discourages both production integration between the region's economies and their participation in global value chains.

Figure 7
Selected country groupings: average cost of trade within the grouping and with the United States (excluding tariffs), 2008-2013
(Percentage tariff equivalents)

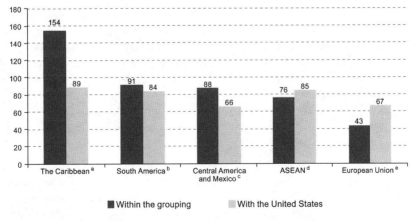

■ Within the grouping   ■ With the United States

Source: Economic Commission for Latin America and the Caribbean (ECLAC), on the basis of information from the World Bank/Economic and Social Commission for Asia and the Pacific (ESCAP), International Trade Costs database [online] http://databank.worldbank.org/data/reports.aspx?source=escap-world-bank:-international-trade-costs.
a Dominican Republic and Jamaica.
b Argentina, Brazil, Chile and Colombia.
c Costa Rica, Guatemala and Mexico.
d Indonesia, Malaysia, the Philippines and Thailand.
e France, Germany and the United Kingdom.

[1]   See [online] http://gtad.wto.org/trta_subcategory.aspx?lg=en&cat=33121.

Between November 2014 and July 2015, ECLAC carried out a survey on the implementation of trade facilitation measures among government bodies in the region, particularly customs authorities and ministries of trade and industry. The results show that the region has made considerable progress on this front, scoring a regional average of 68% on implementation, which is close to the results of Asian countries that took part in the Global Survey, such as India, Malaysia and the Philippines.

The region's relatively high score overall masks significant subregional differences, especially between South America and Central America and Mexico, on the one hand, and the Caribbean, on the other. While the average implementation rate in South America and Central America and Mexico was over 70%, in the Caribbean was barely over 50%. The country with the highest score in the Caribbean (the Dominican Republic) trailed some 10 percentage points behind the top scorers in South America and Central America and Mexico (Colombia and Mexico, respectively). The Caribbean economy with the lowest implementation rate (Suriname) scored almost 20 percentage points below its counterpart in South America (Plurinational State of Bolivia) and nearly 30 percentage points below the lowest scorer in Central America and Mexico (Nicaragua) (see figure 8).

Figure 8
Latin America and the Caribbean (19 countries): total scores in the Global Survey on Trade Facilitation and Paperless Trade Implementation 2015
(Percentages of maximum possible score)

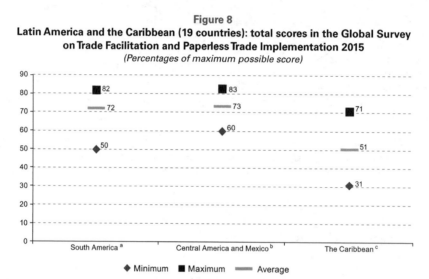

◆ Minimum   ■ Maximum   ▬ Average

Source: Economic Commission for Latin America and the Caribbean (ECLAC), on the basis of information from the Global Survey on Trade Facilitation and Paperless Trade Implementation 2015.
[a] Brazil, Chile, Colombia, Ecuador, Paraguay, Peru, Plurinational State of Bolivia and Uruguay.
[b] Costa Rica, El Salvador, Guatemala, Honduras, Mexico, Nicaragua and Panama.
[c] Barbados, Dominican Republic, Suriname, and Trinidad and Tobago.

The relatively high implementation rates in Central American countries are largely the result of a common legal framework, the Uniform Central American Customs Code (CAUCA), which has permitted harmonization and simplification of export and import procedures and cross-border electronic sharing of documentation. Another factor has been the signing by Central American countries of a free trade agreement with the United States (the Dominican Republic-Central America-United States Free Trade Agreement (CAFTA-DR)) and an association agreement with the European Union (to which Panama is also a signatory). Both instruments contain chapters on trade facilitation that are broad in scope. A significant role is also played by international cooperation received by Central American countries in the area of trade facilitation.

In South America, Colombia, Ecuador, Chile, Brazil and Peru have the highest implementation rates. As is the case for the Central American countries, Chile, Colombia and Peru have free trade agreements with the United States and the European Union, which include broad trade facilitation provisions. Ecuador has implemented the ECUAPASS computer system (based on the UNI-PASS system in the Republic of Korea), which has enabled almost all customs procedures to be digitalized.

The results for the Caribbean show that the challenges faced by the subregion are different to those of the rest of the region, including the island status and small size of the subregion's economies, the limited availability of air and sea connections between them and high levels of public debt that restrict the fiscal space to invest in modernizing foreign trade procedures. Against this backdrop, the Caribbean Community (CARICOM) has established a regional aid for trade strategy, which aims to secure international cooperation resources for a limited number of high-impact initiatives, including several related to trade facilitation.

The region's progress varies widely depending on the type of measure implemented. On the whole, the highest scores were obtained in relation to the category of transparency, which includes establishing independent appeals mechanisms for challenging customs rulings, publishing legislation and regulations on the Internet and issuing advance rulings on tariff classification. By contrast, the least progress was recorded on measures involving the cross-border electronic sharing of documentation, such as certificates of origin and sanitary certificates (see table 1). This is because sharing documentation electronically across borders requires not only sophisticated information and communications technology infrastructure, but also a high degree of cooperation and trust among the authorities of the countries sharing that documentation.

Table 1
Latin America and the Caribbean (19 countries): [a] distribution of implementation rates on 30 trade facilitation measures, 2015

Regional implementation rate	Number of measures	Examples
85% and over	8	• Automated customs system • Independent mechanism for appealing customs rulings • Electronic payment of customs duties and other fees • Publication of regulations on the Internet
70% to 84%	10	• Advance rulings on tariff classification • Use of risk management • Pre-arrival processing
50% to 69%	6	• Advance publication of new regulations • Electronic single window system for foreign trade • Facilitation measures for authorized operators
Less than 50%	6	• Electronic application for refunds of customs payments • Cross-border electronic sharing of certificates of origin • Cross-border electronic sharing of sanitary certificates

Source: Economic Commission for Latin America and the Caribbean (ECLAC), on the basis of information from the Global Survey on Trade Facilitation and Paperless Trade Implementation 2015.
[a] Barbados, Brazil, Chile, Colombia, Costa Rica, Dominican Republic, Ecuador, El Salvador, Guatemala, Honduras, Mexico, Nicaragua, Panama, Paraguay, Peru, Plurinational State of Bolivia, Suriname, Trinidad and Tobago, and Uruguay.

Some of the measures in which there has been relatively modest progress across the region do not require substantial financial investments. This is the case for the creation of national trade facilitation committees, the regular publication of average times for release of traded goods and the advance publication of new regulations before they enter into force. The main factors constraining implementation of these measures could be of a political or institutional nature such as, for example, trade facilitation not being perceived as a political priority or some agencies being reluctant to submit to higher standards of transparency and accountability.

The region needs to make progress on the trade facilitation agenda for a number of reasons. Expediting trade flows between its countries would help to increase the levels of intraregional trade. Moreover, since inefficiencies in border procedures disproportionally affect SMEs (the vast majority of which do not export), trade facilitation may promote their internationalization. This, in turn, may encourage export diversification and reduce the region's, and particularly South America's, current dependence on raw materials.

The weakness of regional and global value chains highlights the importance of trade facilitation as a competitiveness factor. If the production of a final good is divided between two or more countries, the number of cross-border transactions increases, in particular for parts, components and other inputs. This, in turn, increases the cost of inefficiencies in document management and administrative procedures at borders. This cost is particularly high in perishable goods chains, those that operate with small inventories and those that must adapt their product specifications quickly to changes in demand.

Progress in trade facilitation could strengthen weak intraregional production chains and increase the region's very limited presence in global value chains. Moreover, several concepts that underpin the trade facilitation agenda, such as making government agencies more transparent and efficient and promoting public-private dialogue, are also crucial for increasing State efficiency and combating corruption.

Although trade facilitation is often seen as relevant only to customs authorities, in practice it concerns many other public bodies that perform border inspections or issue documents required for foreign trade transactions, such as ministries of transport, health and environment and health protection services. The cross-cutting nature of the trade facilitation agenda raises serious institutional challenges for the countries of the region. A great deal of thought must therefore be given to the design of the national trade facilitation committees responsible for implementing the WTO Trade Facilitation Agreement in order to secure a commitment from political authorities and effective public-private coordination.

The survey results show that many countries in the region have made considerable progress, but the impact of that progress would be greater if it were coordinated at the regional or at least the subregional level. For example, if the aim is to ease the operations of regional value chains, it would be preferable for a number of countries to agree among themselves on the criteria a firm has to meet to be considered an authorized operator, or on the content of advance rulings. Similarly, the design of the procedures needed to ensure full interoperability of national single windows for foreign trade should be coordinated at the regional or subregional level. The experience of Central America illustrates the benefits of coordinating with neighbouring countries on these matters. The recent discussions undertaken between the Pacific Alliance and the Southern Common Market (MERCOSUR) with a view to exploring the scope for joint trade facilitation work have great potential to boost trade and productive integration throughout the region.

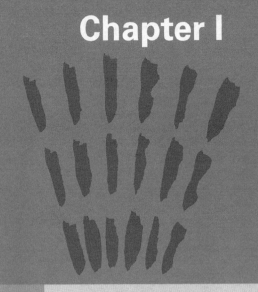

Chapter I

Slow growth and global uncertainty exacerbate the region's weaknesses

A. An international context of slow growth

1. World trade has not recovered since the crisis

Seven years on from the start of the economic and financial crisis of 2008 and 2009, world trade has yet to recover the dynamism it showed during most of the post-war period. The present chapter analyses the factors underlying this and the effects on the external trade of Latin America and the Caribbean.

World trade was very dynamic between 1952 and 2014, with world export volumes growing by more than gross domestic product (GDP) in 52 of the 62 years of the period (see figure I.1). The main factors in this performance were, first, the creation of the General Agreement on Tariffs and Trade (GATT) in 1947, which initiated a multilateral process of reductions in the high trade barriers erected between the wars. Also important was the creation of the European Economic Community (now the European Union) in 1957, followed by successive rounds of enlargement and the establishment of its single market from the 1980s, which invigorated trade between the countries of the continent. Third, the increasing geographical fragmentation of global production from the mid-1980s boosted trade in intermediate products. A fourth factor was the opening of the Chinese economy that began in the late 1970s and the heavily export-oriented development strategy adopted by the Chinese government. These last two factors are interrelated since China is now at the centre of the international network of industrial value chains known as "factory Asia".

World trade was very dynamic in the post-war period

Figure I.1
Annual variations in global goods export volumes and global GDP, 1952-2014
(Percentages)

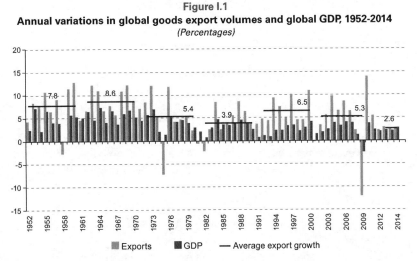

Source: Economic Commission for Latin America and the Caribbean (ECLAC), on the basis of data from the World Trade Organization (WTO) and the International Monetary Fund (IMF).

Trade lost momentum after the global crisis, however, with its growth rate falling below that of output. After dropping by 12% in 2009 and recovering by 14% in 2010, it seems to have plateaued. Between 2012 and 2014, world exports averaged volume growth of only 2.6%, which almost exactly matched the average expansion of the world economy in the same period (2.5%) and was just half the average rate attained in the stage immediately prior to the crisis (2001-2008). World trade looks even more sluggish when measured by value, since the global export price index has only moved downward since 2012 as the prices of commodities, especially oil and metals, have declined (see figure I.2).

The poor performance of world trade since 2012 has been due to a combination of factors, which can be divided into two groups: those linked to the difficult global macroeconomic situation and those related to changes in the dynamics of production and of trade itself. On the macroeconomic level, trade flows have been adversely affected by the persistent weakness of aggregate global demand, despite the expansionary monetary policies applied by the industrialized countries. A number of things have contributed to this situation, which some have even labelled "secular stagnation". They include a surplus of global production capacity in a number of industries, the instability resulting from the decoupling of financial activity from real activity, high levels of public debt in several leading economies, a marked worsening of income distribution in a substantial number of countries, and the slowdown in the Chinese economy combined with uncertainty about when its growth model might be rebalanced.

World trade has lost momentum since the crisis

Figure I.2
Annual variations in global goods exports by value and volume, 1992-2015 [a]
(Percentages)

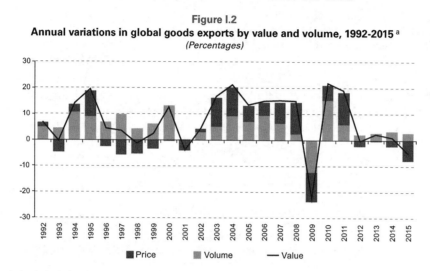

■ Price   ■ Volume   — Value

Source: Economic Commission for Latin America and the Caribbean (ECLAC), on the basis of Netherlands Bureau for Economic Policy Analysis (CPB), World Trade Database [online] http://www.cpb.nl/en/world-trade-monitor.
[a] Figures for 2015 are ECLAC projections based on data from the World Trade Organization (WTO) and the United Nations Commodity Trade Statistics Database (COMTRADE) and price series information for the period from January to August 2015.

Where production and trade are concerned, the rapid fragmentation of production that began in the second half of the 1980s and was a strong driver of world trade, especially for intermediate goods, now appears to have reached a stage of maturity. The new configuration beginning to take shape could result in shorter regional and global value chains, and thence lessened trade dynamism. For example, China has gone a long way towards replacing imported inputs with local ones in a number of industries, thereby reducing the dynamism of world trade in intermediate goods. Meanwhile, a shift towards less import-intensive components in the composition of aggregate global demand since the crisis has also had a negative impact on trade flows.

The rest of this chapter is structured as follows. Subsection A.2 addresses the macroeconomic determinants of the stagnation in world trade, while subsection A.3 concentrates on causes directly bound up with the trade dynamic itself. Section B examines the implications of the international context for the trade of Latin America and the Caribbean and presents projections for 2015. Lastly, section C presents conclusions and some policy recommendations for the region.

2. The macroeconomics of the post-crisis period: structural asymmetries and recessionary adjustment

(a) Too little demand and too much liquidity

The weakness of the global recovery since the crisis has resulted from a combination of real and financial variables, together with imbalances in the international economy and within national economies. In particular, the dynamics of international finance decoupled yet further from that of the real economy in this period. In the years leading up to the crisis, external financial assets grew much more quickly than GDP, gross fixed capital formation or goods and services exports, and the gap widened after the crisis (see figure I.3). This trend can be seen as a classic case of a Keynesian liquidity trap, with plentiful international liquidity as yet unmatched by a vigorous response from aggregate demand.

Finance has decoupled from the real economy

Figure I.3
External financial assets [a] and selected real variables worldwide, 2003-2013
(Indices, 2003=100) [b]

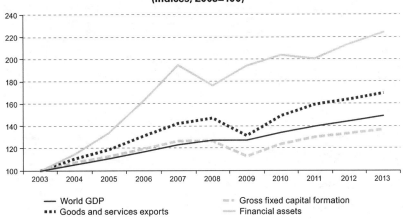

Source: Economic Commission for Latin America and the Caribbean (ECLAC), on the basis of data from the International Monetary Fund (IMF), the United Nations Conference on Trade and Development (UNCTAD) and the World Bank.
[a] Calculated on the basis of each country's international investment position.
[b] All indices are calculated in 2005 dollars.

The growth in countries' external financial assets is a corollary of the rising current account imbalances that have built up in the world's leading economies. Figure I.4 shows the distribution of imbalances between countries, as represented by their balance-of-payments current account situation, and the substantial growth in these from 2002 right up to the crisis. Two things stand out: the reduction of the United States deficit in the post-crisis period, associated with lower growth and a falling fiscal deficit, and persistent surpluses in China, oil-exporting countries and Germany and the rest of Europe. The size of the German surplus has increased over time, and whereas it was due to trade with the country's European partners in the years leading up to the crisis, since then it has increasingly been generated by trade with the rest of the world as the European economy has stagnated. The combined surplus of Germany and the Netherlands was greater than China's in 2013 and in the next two-year period, offsetting the positive effect on global balances of the decline in the Chinese surplus after 2008. Latin America and the Caribbean went back into deficit with the end of the commodity boom.

The sign of the different countries' current account balances tends to be fairly stable. The automatic mechanisms of rising effective demand or declining competitiveness in surplus countries (via real exchange-rate appreciation and higher real wages) have not acted strongly enough to restore balance to the international economy. Fearing inflation, an overheating labour market, rising public debt or loss of the positions they have won for themselves in external markets, surplus countries have proven reluctant to pursue expansionary fiscal policies that would increase their imports and raise wages.

For emerging economies, including those of the region, it is hard to increase exports, output and investment when the markets of the major developed economies are not expanding. If the latter apply recessionary policies, emerging economies will have to make large adjustments, with all the economic and social costs entailed. There is thus a need for policy coordination in the global economy in pursuit of simultaneous expansion in surplus and deficit countries, facilitated by the tendency towards trade reciprocity.[1]

---

[1]   The concept of trade reciprocity was used by Raúl Prebisch to stress the need for the central countries to favour the exports of peripheral economies, thereby boosting their growth. See [online] http://archivo.cepal.org/pdfs/cdPrebisch/076.pdf.

Imbalances and their distribution: recessionary adjustment

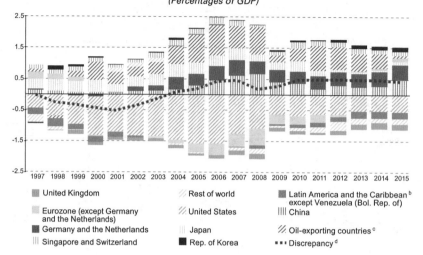

Figure I.4
Selected groupings and countries: balance-of-payments current account balances, 1997-2015 [a]
(Percentages of GDP)

Legend:
- United Kingdom
- Eurozone (except Germany and the Netherlands)
- Germany and the Netherlands
- Singapore and Switzerland
- Rest of world
- United States
- Japan
- Rep. of Korea
- Latin America and the Caribbean [b] except Venezuela (Bol. Rep. of)
- China
- Oil-exporting countries [c]
- Discrepancy [d]

Source: Economic Commission for Latin America and the Caribbean (ECLAC), on the basis of International Monetary Fund (IMF), *2015 External Sector Report*, Washington, D.C., 27 July 2015 and other IMF information.

[a] Figures for 2015 are projections.
[b] Argentina, Brazil, Chile, Colombia, Costa Rica, the Dominican Republic, El Salvador, Ecuador, Guatemala, Honduras, Mexico, Panama, Paraguay, Peru, the Plurinational State of Bolivia, Trinidad and Tobago and Uruguay.
[c] Algeria, Angola, the Bolivarian Republic of Venezuela, Canada, the Islamic Republic of Iran, Kuwait, Libya, Nigeria, Norway, Qatar, the Russian Federation and Saudi Arabia.
[d] The statistical discrepancy line quantifies the difference between the cumulative surpluses and deficits, which by definition ought to cancel out.

The logic prevailing in the dynamics of the international economy thus has a recessionary bias, since the whole weight of adjustment is falling on deficit countries, which are having to accept slower growth or economic contraction. With the exception of the United States, which issues the international reserve currency, countries cannot run large current account deficits for long. Many deficit countries evince substantial productivity shortfalls that are limiting the positive effects of currency depreciation on exports, so that adjustment is taking place via imports and resulting in lower growth. This form of adjustment carries major risks, since lower output growth also means lower investment, weakening these countries' export and productivity performance yet further.

These disequilibria have led to differences in the way countries perceive the problem, depending on whether they are in surplus or deficit. Surplus countries tend to view their trading partners' deficits as a manifestation not of technological and productive asymmetries, but of excess spending. Private borrowing is usually the source of the imbalances, but these debts are then taken over by the State to forestall a possible systemic crisis resulting from financial sector collapse. In consequence, adjustments become primarily fiscal and the debate focuses on austerity in the public sector. In a world of too little aggregate demand and too much liquidity, this reinforces the recessionary bias in the international system. Perceptions have shifted over recent years, and the adoption of an expansionary fiscal stimulus by surplus countries (combined with debt relief in deficit countries) is starting to be regarded by analysts as a more effective countercyclical policy option (Summers, 2014; Blanchard, 2015).

The decoupling of financial products has compounded the imbalances originating in the real economy. The ability of global financial markets to mobilize and leverage resources makes it extremely difficult for governments to act to stop bubbles inflating, control speculation in currencies and commodities and limit the non-bank borrowing and shadow banking systems that elude or operate outside of prudential rules. The growing role of financial markets and institutions has been manifested, in particular, in the exponential growth of financial assets, far outstripping growth in real activity. The value of the global stock of such assets was the equivalent of 29% of world GDP in 1980, but was almost twice as great in 1990 and 12 times as great by 2013 (see figure I.5).

The greater role of the financial sector and its institutions in the workings of economies is also reflected in the degree to which they have brought other markets traditionally associated with real activity in the economy into their sphere of action (i.e., real activity has become financial). This was exemplified by trends in the commodity market in the 2000s, when commodities became a financial asset, with their prices increasingly responding to changes in expectations about future conditions rather than the current state of the market and of supply and demand.

Leverage has risen even since the crisis

Figure I.5
Nominal GDP, financial assets and derivatives worldwide, 1990-2013
(Trillions of dollars)

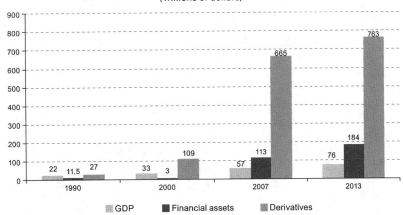

Source: Economic Commission for Latin America and the Caribbean (ECLAC), on the basis of Bank for International Settlements (BIS) and World Bank, World Development Indicators, 2015.

The proliferation of financial assets has greatly increased the risk of crises in deficit economies. For one thing, it has increased the potential for public and private borrowing, being an additional incentive for such borrowing in favourable periods, for example when interest rates are falling. For another, when a shock depresses expectations of growth and solvency in indebted countries, there is a large-scale exit from assets that deepens the contraction and makes it harder to implement growth stabilization and recovery policies.

(b) Excess saving, secular stagnation and debt

The rapid growth of financial assets is connected to the growing scale of public and private debt in the world's leading economies, especially developed ones. The global debt stock rose from 246% of world GDP in 2000 to 269% in 2007 and 286% in 2014 (McKinsey Global Institute, 2015). Growth in public debt and the consequent reduction of fiscal space in the world's leading economies have limited the scope for using public spending as a countercyclical instrument, in a context where monetary policy has brought interest rates down to near or even below zero.

Governments responded to the crisis of 2008 and 2009 with a combination of expansionary fiscal and monetary policies that prevented it from becoming even deeper or more protracted. As fiscal space diminished (because public debt increased as a share of GDP or, in the United States, because of the political problems involved in raising expenditure), the predominant course of action was an expansionary monetary policy in the form of quantitative easing, adopted first by the United States and Japan and more recently by the European Union. Quantitative easing has helped to keep interest rates very low (see figure I.6), but with no acceleration of inflation (see figure I.7). Despite strong monetary expansion, aggregate demand has not picked up significantly (see figure I.8), which confirms the pattern of abundant liquidity and little effective demand (Kregel, 2014).

The combination of low inflation, real interest rates very close to or even below zero and low growth in the global economy has created a savings glut or a situation of secular stagnation. These two concepts are related, in that a glut of savings necessarily implies that there is no portfolio of productive investments attractive enough to absorb them (Bernanke, 2005; Krugman, 2015; Summers, 2015). It also implies excess installed capacity relative to the weak growth of consumption and effective demand in general. Thus, utilization rates in the United States and the European Union have not returned to pre-crisis levels, let alone those of the 1990s (see figure I.9).

Monetary policy has been running out of space

Figure I.6
Selected groupings and countries: policy interest rates, 2000-2015
(Percentages)

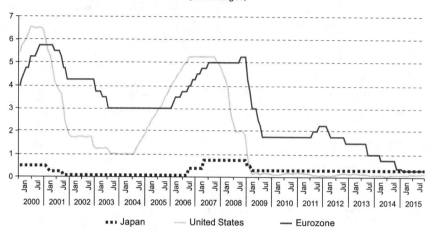

Source: Economic Commission for Latin America and the Caribbean (ECLAC), on the basis of Federal Reserve Bank of St. Louis, Federal Reserve Economic Data (FRED) [online] https://research.stlouisfed.org/fred2/.

Despite quantitative easing, inflation has stayed very low

Figure I.7
Selected groupings and countries: inflation rates, 2000-2015
(Percentages)

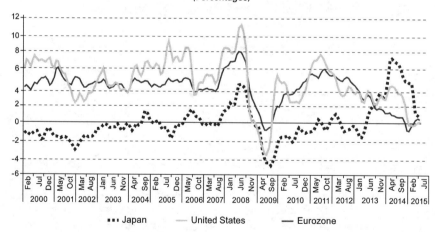

Source: Economic Commission for Latin America and the Caribbean (ECLAC), on the basis of data from the Statistical Bureau of Japan and Federal Reserve Bank of St. Louis, Federal Reserve Economic Data (FRED) [online] https://research.stlouisfed.org/fred2/.

Domestic demand has been less dynamic since the crisis

Figure I.8
**Selected groupings and countries: GDP growth rates and contribution
of aggregate demand components to growth, 2000-2014**
(Percentages)

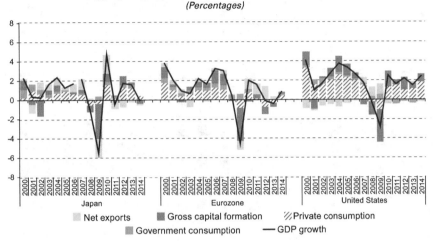

Source: Economic Commission for Latin America and the Caribbean (ECLAC), on the basis of data from the Organization for Economic Cooperation and Development (OECD).

Utilization levels have not recovered

Figure I.9
United States and eurozone: installed capacity utilization, 1990-2015
(Percentages)

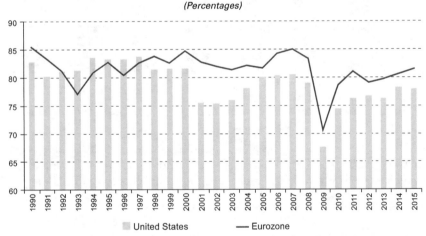

Source: Economic Commission for Latin America and the Caribbean (ECLAC), on the basis of data from Eurostat and the United States Federal Reserve.

This assessment is also relevant at the sectoral level. In processing industries such as copper refining, global capacity utilization since the crisis has been sharply lower than in the period prior to 2008 and 2009. One clear example in Latin America is Brazil's automotive industry, where capacity utilization is expected to drop to 50% in 2016 (see figure I.10). These examples reinforce the idea that global growth will be slow, since no major increases in business investment can be expected at these utilization levels.

The effects of continuing low levels of utilization can be seen in different sectors

Figure I.10
**Installed capacity utilization in global copper refining
and the Brazilian automotive industry**
(Percentages)

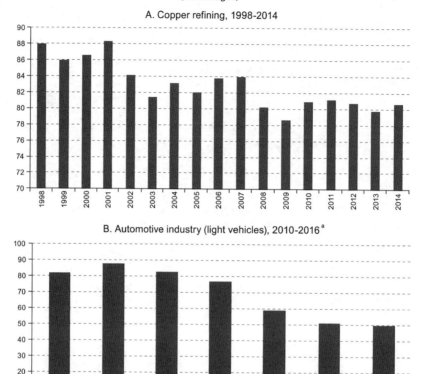

A. Copper refining, 1998-2014

B. Automotive industry (light vehicles), 2010-2016 [a]

Source: Economic Commission for Latin America and the Caribbean (ECLAC), on the basis of Statista [online] www.statista.com and International Copper Study Group (ICSG) [online] www.icsg.org.
[a] Figures for 2015 and 2016 are projections.

There is also overproduction in most sectors producing commodities, particularly inputs for industry, as reflected in their falling prices (World Bank 2015a; EIU, 2015). This development has been particularly marked for energy sources, especially oil, followed by metals. Agricultural and food product prices have also dropped, although by less.

Problems with aggregate demand and surplus capacity have been compounded by other factors limiting investment. It has been argued that the growing weight of government regulations may have increased business costs and reduced the number of profitable investment packages, even with historically low interest rates. Then there are factors deriving from the ongoing technological revolution, particularly increased uncertainty and a decline in long-term productivity growth.

New technologies destroy, reshape or create markets when they permeate the whole of the economic fabric. By shortening product and process life cycles, they increase uncertainty about the returns to be expected from investments in activities directly affected by them. Consequently, firms with a limited ability to process this uncertainty (the great majority) may react by postponing their investment plans. This has a particular impact on countries which are well behind the technology frontier, since for them technical change is essentially exogenous, and on those where there is a large productivity gap between large and small firms.

A production structure with weak knowledge intensity plus the dynamics of the technological revolution explain, in part, why the exports of emerging countries whose currencies have depreciated have not gained competitiveness to the extent that might be expected. These depreciations, resulting in the short term from lower export prices, the strengthening United States dollar and the return of capital to the developed countries (see figure I.11), have accelerated inflationary tendencies and pushed real wages down, with all the negative consequences this has for poverty and inequality.

With the exception of the renminbi, emerging-market currencies have been depreciating

Figure I.11
Selected countries: nominal exchange rates, 2000-2015
(Indices, January 2000=100)

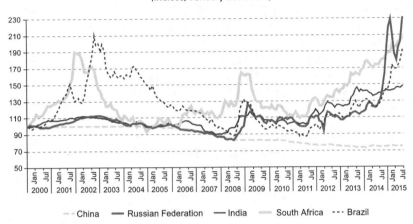

Source: Economic Commission for Latin America and the Caribbean (ECLAC), on the basis of figures from the International Monetary Fund (IMF), the Federal Reserve Bank of St. Louis and the Central Bank of the Russian Federation.

The exports of emerging economies have slowed sharply or fallen since 2011, even though their currencies have depreciated (see figure I.12). This has happened mainly in countries specializing in the export of commodities or commodity-based manufactures. China's export growth has also been slowing (although it has not halted) because of lower prices and lower demand from its trading partners. The United States Federal Reserve has been paying attention to this weakness in the currencies and trade of most emerging countries and other developing countries, expressing its concern about the effects that a normalization of its interest rate might have on them (Fischer, 2015).

Despite currency depreciation, exports from the BRICS have fallen

Figure I.12
Selected countries: annual variations in exports by value, 2001-2005
(Percentages)

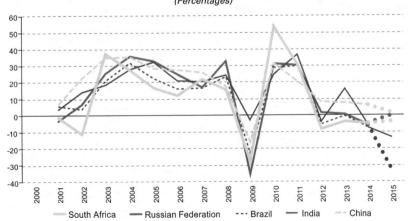

Source: Economic Commission for Latin America and the Caribbean (ECLAC), on the basis of the United Nations Commodity Trade Statistics Database (COMTRADE).

There seems to be a relationship between the weakness of effective demand and the marked rise in the inequality of income distribution in many countries. In the member countries of the Organization for Economic Cooperation and Development (OECD) as a group, the ratio between the incomes of the richest 10% of the population and the poorest 10% has risen continuously from 7 to 1 in the 1980s to 9.6 to 1 now (OECD, 2015a). Although inequality has fallen over the period in some developing countries, especially in Latin America (ECLAC, 2013b), it remains much higher there than in the industrialized countries. Worsening income distribution has meant a relative decline in the purchasing power of much of the population and driven family borrowing higher, with an important role having been played in this by rising home prices, a key factor in many recent financial bubbles.

In summary, the real economy stagnated after the crisis, while financialization encouraged higher public and private borrowing. In this context, weak aggregate demand and surplus production capacity led the monetary authorities of the developed economies to increase liquidity. Recovery in the United States followed an initial depreciation of the dollar that improved the country's competitiveness and reduced its trade deficit. Although adjustment in the eurozone also involved lower imports, euro depreciation and increased international competitiveness, recession and unemployment have been much more persistent there. In the third major actor, China, the export-based model came up against problems and growth slowed substantially.

(c) China's transition to its new development model is impacting the world economy

China achieved average annual GDP growth of close to 10% from the 1980s until the financial crisis of 2008 and 2009. However, the model followed for over three decades shows signs of running its course, and the growth rate has fallen back since then to 7.4% in 2014. Other economic indicators have also shown a declining trend (see figure I.13).

Economic activity has been slowing quickly in China

Figure I.13
China: annual variations in selected economic indicators [a]
(Percentages)

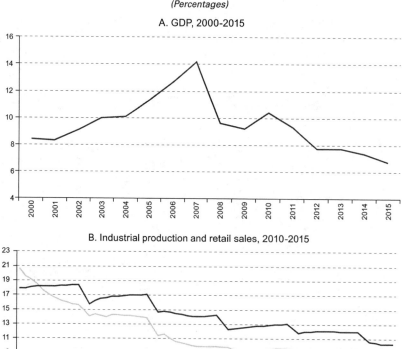

A. GDP, 2000-2015

B. Industrial production and retail sales, 2010-2015

Industrial production — Retail sales

Figure I.13 (concluded)

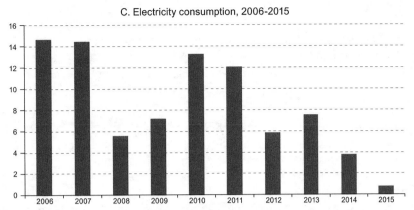

C. Electricity consumption, 2006-2015

Source: Economic Commission for Latin America and the Caribbean (ECLAC), on the basis of International Monetary Fund (IMF), World Economic Outlook Database, April 2015 (for GDP), the National Bureau of Statistics of China (for industrial production and retail sales) and the National Energy Administration of China (for electricity consumption).
^a Figures for 2015 are projections, except in the case of electricity consumption, where the figure is for the January to July period.

The Chinese model heavily encouraged saving as a mechanism for financing high investment rates, as a result of which consumption as a share of output was low. The model was also heavily oriented towards manufacturing exports, with a large (but declining) imported content: the ratio between Chinese part and component imports and manufacturing exports peaked at about 75% in the mid-1990s and fell to 35% by 2012 (Constantinescu, Mattoo and Ruta, 2015).

China's growth model has created growing imbalances, especially since the crisis, that have compromised its continuing viability. First, investment in infrastructure, industry and housing, which accounted for almost half of GDP growth in the last decade, was largely financed by increasing borrowing (ECLAC, 2015). Public debt tripled and private debt quadrupled between 2008 and 2014. Since nominal GDP only doubled in the period, total debt as a share of GDP rose from 150% to 235% (see figure I.14). Furthermore, some components of this borrowing have increased instability: property speculation, the large debts of local governments and the strong presence of shadow banking in the financial sector (McKinsey Global Institute, 2015).

China's total debt has multiplied since the crisis

Figure I.14
China: public and private debt, 2000-2014
(Trillions of dollars and percentages of GDP)

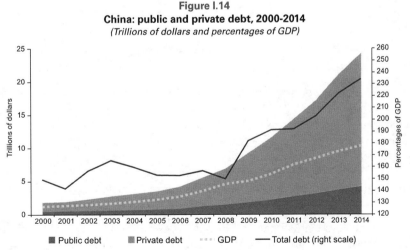

Source: Economic Commission for Latin America and the Caribbean (ECLAC), on the basis of figures from the Bank for International Settlements (BIS) and the International Monetary Fund (IMF).

Secondly, the high investment rate led to overcapacity in a number of industries, such as steel, cement, glass and electrical equipment (ECLAC, 2015). Third, this overinvestment resulted in a decline in capital returns, efficiency and productivity, and in lower total factor productivity (Cros, 2015). Other strains in the model are the growing disparity between growth in coastal and inland areas of the country and severe environmental damage.

Another effect of high saving and investment was to create bubbles in the property sector and, more recently, the stock market. The first bubble inflated between 2005 and the first half of 2013. Home prices rose at very high rates until the government took measures that reversed this trend in the second half of 2013. The price fall continued until late 2014 (World Bank, 2015c). A less attractive real estate sector meant that some savings were diverted into the Shanghai stock market, creating another bubble, with the market rising by about 150% between June 2014 and June 2015. However, predictions of lower economic growth, capital outflows from the country and a mini-devaluation of the renminbi resulted in a sharp correction (41%) in July and August 2015. The government took a number of measures that forestalled a larger drop in the short term.

The Chinese growth model has heavily influenced the structure of the world economy. Rising investment and exports were very intensive in commodity imports. In the last decade, China has become the leading consumer (over 40% of the worldwide total in 2014) of a number of commodities such as aluminium, coal, copper, iron and soya. The resulting rise in prices for these reversed in 2013 and 2014, and the prices of industrial products, for which China has a surplus of installed capacity, also fell (see figure I.15).[2] Thus, the country contributed heavily to the global excess capacity affecting a number of industries. Lower international demand for the industrial goods exported by China has also contributed to the unsustainability of the model.

Excess capacity has caused industrial product prices to plummet

Figure I.15
China: annual variations in producer prices, 2000-2015 [a]
(Percentages)

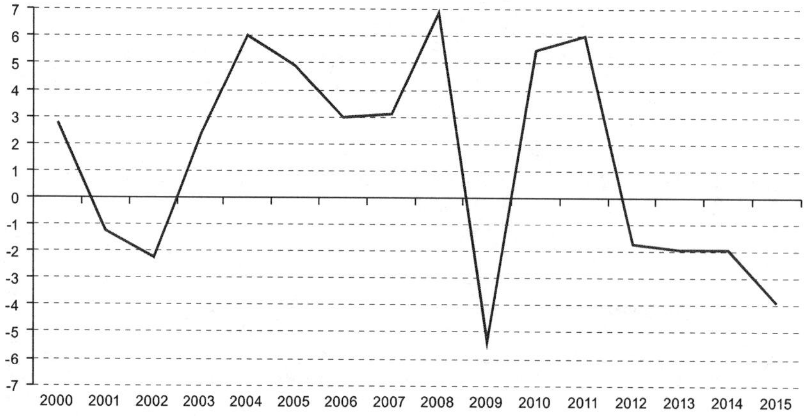

Source: Economic Commission for Latin America and the Caribbean (ECLAC), on the basis of figures from the International Monetary Fund (IMF).
[a] The 2015 figure is a projection by the Economist Intelligence Unit (EIU).

Aware of the limitations of their growth model, the Chinese authorities initiated a process of rebalancing in the economy with a view to moving gradually towards slower and more sustainable growth based on urbanization, private consumption and services. The purpose of the rebalancing is to correct the problems mentioned and promote social stability and environmental protection by achieving growth that is more intensive in job creation in services and intangibles, with less emphasis on physical capital formation. Some of the main economic variables have started to respond to these changes. In 2014, services represented 48% of the economy (4 percentage points more than in 2010) and urban employment increased by 13 million workers (3 million more than the government target). In turn, the annual investment growth rate slowed to about 6% (ECLAC, 2015; OECD, 2015b).

The transition to the new normal is complex. Private consumption is not yet dynamic enough to meet the growth targets set by the government and replace lower demand from investment and exports. Furthermore, private consumption is harder for the government to stimulate than public investment. Consumers are not increasing their spending quickly and are maintaining fairly high saving rates, in a context where public social services (education,

2   The collapse of the Shanghai stock exchange in July and August 2015 led to a further fall in commodity prices and a depreciation of over 10% against the dollar for the currencies of several commodity-exporting countries.

pensions and health care) are limited and the population is ageing. Against this background, the central bank has cut its main interest rate and minimum bank capital requirements to promote consumer lending. Meanwhile, some measures designed to resolve imbalances, such as greater control over the informal banking system, which accounts for a third of all loans, and over lending to local authorities, are negatively affecting growth.

The world economy has struggled to adapt to slower growth in China. For one thing, lower demand for commodity exports (except in the case of agricultural products) has been affecting the countries that export those products by way of lower prices and volumes, causing their currencies to depreciate substantially. For another, countries producing manufactured parts and components that participate in factory Asia have also been affected by lower Chinese demand. The global deflationary impact has been heightened by the recent devaluation of the renminbi against the dollar, which has increased uncertainty about the future path of the currency (see figure I.16).

In August 2015, the renminbi was devalued slightly

Figure I.16
Nominal exchange rate of the renminbi against the dollar,
January 2005 to August 2015
(Inverted scale)

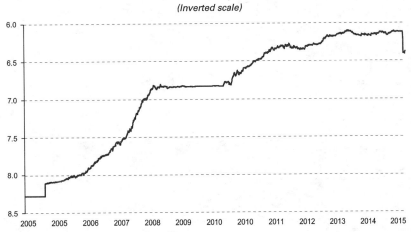

Source: Economic Commission for Latin America and the Caribbean (ECLAC), on the basis of International Monetary Fund (IMF), World Economic Outlook Database, April 2015.

Between 2003 and 2014, China built up reserves totalling US$ 4 trillion. Some of these were invested in United States Treasury Bonds, making China the largest holder of these bonds outside the United States (US$ 1.3 trillion as of June 2015). However, the situation has started to change in recent months because of steady capital outflows associated with the slackening of the economy. Furthermore, devaluation has created negative expectations about the stability of the Chinese financial system and resulted in large losses of international reserves, as the central bank has sold United States Treasury Bonds and dollars to support the currency. A clear contradiction has thus arisen between the desirability of devaluation to restore competitiveness and the country's goal of turning the renminbi into a reserve currency.

All this illustrates the difficulty of moving from a model based on investment and exports to one oriented more towards domestic consumption, in a context of greater financial liberalization, greater private-sector involvement in public enterprises, capital account opening and a more flexible exchange rate. The rising cost of labour, the deterioration of income distribution and lower population growth are also intensifying the domestic constraints on growth and complicating the transition to a model based more on the domestic market.

3. The changing dynamics of global trade are impeding its recovery

The expansion of international trade has been negatively affected by slow growth in the economies of the European Union since the crisis, an effect that has been particularly large because of their significant share of world exports and imports: a third of the total, if trade between European Union member States is included (see figure I.17). With economic activity in the European Union having been depressed for several years, its demand for imports has also been sluggish, affecting global trade because of the large share of exports that go to it from the European Union member countries themselves (63%), the United States (17%) and China (16%). The shortfall has not been made up by emerging economies such as China, India and Brazil, whose shares of world imports are much smaller (10%, 2% and 1%, respectively).

The European Union still accounts for a third of world trade

Figure I.17
Selected regions and countries: shares of world trade, 2000 and 2014
(Percentages)

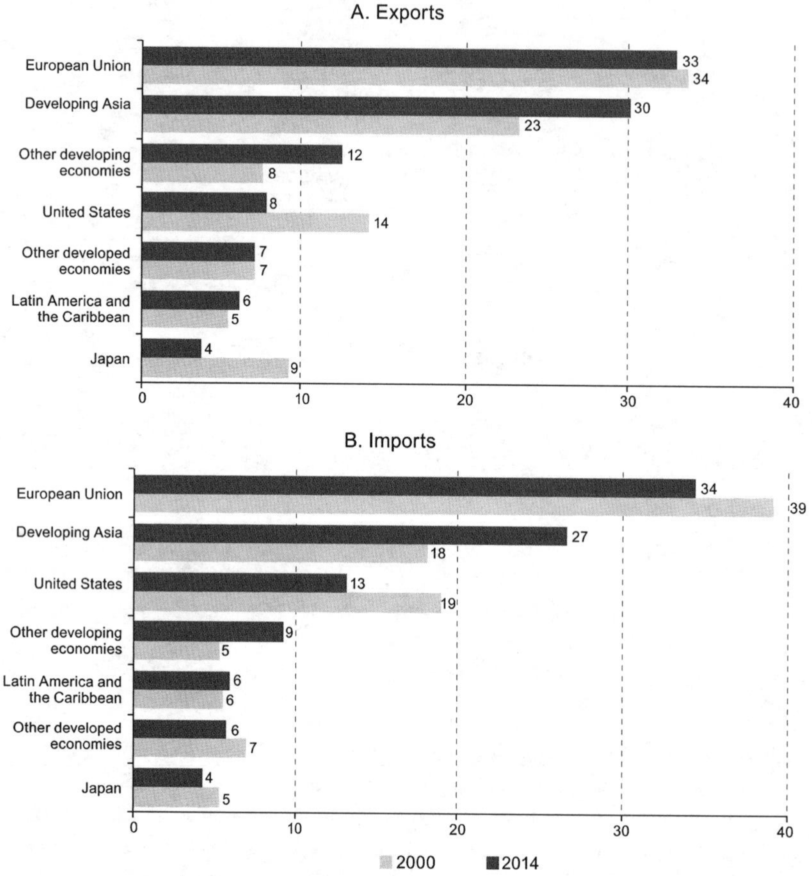

A. Exports

Region	2000	2014
European Union	34	33
Developing Asia	23	30
Other developing economies	8	12
United States	14	8
Other developed economies	7	7
Latin America and the Caribbean	5	6
Japan	9	4

B. Imports

Region	2000	2014
European Union	39	34
Developing Asia	18	27
United States	19	13
Other developing economies	5	9
Latin America and the Caribbean	6	6
Other developed economies	7	6
Japan	5	4

2000 2014

Source: Economic Commission for Latin America and the Caribbean (ECLAC), on the basis of the United Nations Commodity Trade Statistics Database (COMTRADE).

Another factor checking the dynamism of trade has been the shift in the structure of aggregate demand since the crisis, as investment has been less dynamic than private consumption or government spending. Because these last two components are less import-intensive than aggregate demand, trade growth has been slower. This development has been heightened by lower private consumption of durable goods, with many consumers putting off purchases of these in a context of low growth and high uncertainty (Constantinescu, Mattoo and Ruta, 2015; Francis and Morel, 2015).

In the third place, the incentives for geographical fragmentation of production created by the integration of eastern Europe and China into the world economy appear to be dwindling. The fall of the Berlin wall and subsequent integration of the eastern European countries into the economic dynamic of the continent boosted trade and the development of European value chains. Similarly, the opening up of China and its adoption of a strongly export-oriented development model set in train an intensive process that saw production activities relocated in Asia and the rest of the world, giving a boost to world trade. Both of these processes, and thence the impetus they have given world trade, would seem to be running their course (Constantinescu, Mattoo and Ruta, 2015; Francis and Morel, 2015). For example, rising real wages in China have reduced the incentives to move production to the country. Indeed, there has been incipient reshoring of certain manufacturing activities in the United States and some European countries in response to lower energy costs, the reduction of wage differences with China and problems deriving from the separation between technological research and development (R&D) and manufacturing processes.

In the fourth place, global trade flows are being negatively affected because Chinese exporters are gradually substituting imported inputs for locally produced ones, something they have been able to do thanks to a long process of capacity-building and scaling-up within global value chains. An analysis based on data for international trade in value added shows a reduction in the share represented by imported inputs in Chinese exports, from 37% in 2005 to 32% in 2011. This contrasts with a rising share of imported inputs in the external sales of the world's other three largest exporters, the United States, Germany and Japan (see figure I.18), over the same period. The reduction in the content of imported parts and components in Chinese industrial exports, as presented in the previous section, confirms this import substitution process, which has been going on for as long as two decades.

China is reducing the imported component of its exports

Figure I.18
Selected countries: imported content in goods and services exports,
1995, 2005 and 2011
(Percentages)

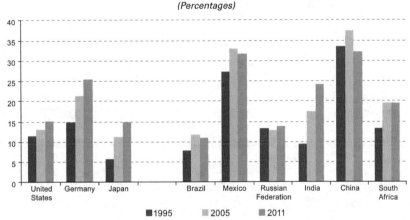

Source: Economic Commission for Latin America and the Caribbean (ECLAC), on the basis of Organization for Economic Cooperation and Development (OECD)/ World Trade Organization (WTO), Trade in Value Added (TiVA) database.

Medium- and high-technology Chinese manufacturing sectors have led the substitution of imported inputs with domestically produced ones. The high-technology industry, which mainly produces information and communications technology equipment, underwent one of the most intensive processes of geographical fragmentation in the 1990s. China was one of the main beneficiaries of this, with many multinationals in the sector moving there. In 1995, three quarters of the value of goods exported by China in this sector consisted of imported inputs. Over the following 16 years, the share dropped to 55% (see figure I.19). Much the same happened in industries producing goods with a medium-high and low technology component.

The world trade impact of import substitution in China's high-technology industry has been magnified by the fact that this segment accounts for much of the rise in Chinese exports to advanced markets, with the composition of imports from China in the United States, Japan and the European Union having shown a substantial shift from low-technology to high-technology goods (see figure I.20).

Besides the causes already mentioned for the slowdown in world trade, there are others, usually deemed less important. They include reduced access to trade financing since the crisis broke out (especially for SMEs), a rise in protectionist measures (usually non-tariff) and greater awareness of the risks posed by the international fragmentation of production because of natural disasters, such as the earthquake in Japan and the flooding in Thailand in 2011.

China is particularly reducing the imported content of medium- and high-technology exports

Figure I.19
China: imported content of exports by sector, 1995, 2005 and 2011
(Percentages)

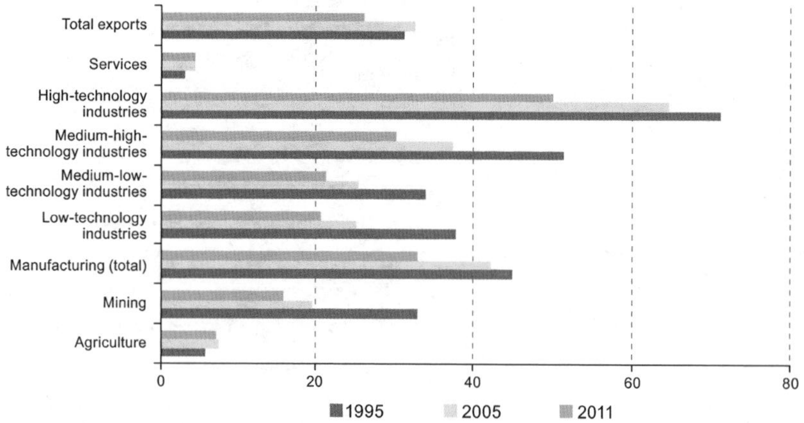

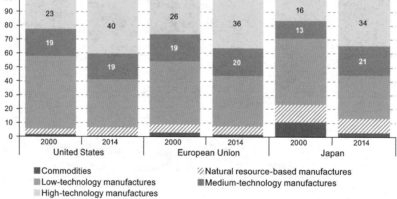

■1995   2005   ■2011

Source: Economic Commission for Latin America and the Caribbean (ECLAC), on the basis of Organization for Economic Cooperation and Development (OECD)/ World Trade Organization (WTO), Trade in Value Added (TiVA) database.

High-technology products are increasing their share in the industrialized countries' imports from China

Figure I.20
United States, European Union and Japan: structure of goods imports from China, 2000 and 2014
(Percentages)

■ Commodities   ⁄⁄Natural resource-based manufactures
■ Low-technology manufactures   ■ Medium-technology manufactures
■ High-technology manufactures

Source: Economic Commission for Latin America and the Caribbean (ECLAC), on the basis of the United Nations Commodity Trade Statistics Database (COMTRADE).

The slowdown in world trade following the crisis of 2008 and 2009 coincided with the start of several trade negotiations with a vast geographical, economic and thematic scope, known as "mega-regional" negotiations (ECLAC, 2013a). If these negotiations are successful, the results could inject greater dynamism into world trade in the coming years. These agreements include the Trans-Pacific Partnership (TPP) Agreement, the Transatlantic Trade and Investment Partnership (TTIP) between the United States and the European Union, and the Regional Comprehensive Economic Partnership (RCEP), which involves the largest Asian economies. Three of the region's countries —Chile, Mexico and Peru— participated in the TPP negotiations, which were concluded recently (see box I.1).

Box I.1
The Trans-Pacific Partnership Agreement

On 5 October 2015, the successful conclusion of the negotiations on the Trans-Pacific Partnership Agreement (TPP) was announced. This process, which was formally launched in 2010, has paved the way for creating the world's largest free trade area, to be made up of 12 countries: Australia, Brunei Darussalam, Canada, Chile, Japan, Malaysia, Mexico, New Zealand, Peru, Singapore, the United States and Viet Nam. In 2014, this group, which includes 5 of the world's 20 largest economies, accounted for 36% of world GDP (in current dollars), 23% of world goods exports, 26% of imports, 28% of foreign direct investment (FDI) inflows, 43% of FDI outflows, and 11% of the world population.

Trade between the members of the TPP amounted to US$ 2.1 trillion and constituted 48% of total exports and 40% of total imports for this group of countries in 2014. The importance of the TPP as a trading partner varies widely among its members, including the three Latin American member countries. The TPP accounts for about one third of total trade for Chile and Peru, measured by both exports and imports, but a much larger proportion for Mexico since the United States is the primary destination for Mexican exports. In 2014, the United States accounted for 94% of Mexican exports to the countries of the TPP and was the source of 83% of its imports from these countries.

Chile, Mexico and Peru: share of the Trans-Pacific Partnership in total goods trade, 2014
(Percentages)

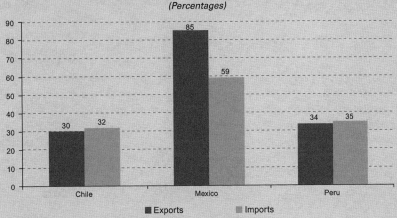

Source: Economic Commission for Latin America and the Caribbean (ECLAC), on the basis of the United Nations Commodity Trade Statistics Database (COMTRADE).

To date, the text of the agreement has not been disclosed publicly. However, the thematic scope of the agreement is vast and includes not only the elimination of tariffs for most trade in goods between its members, but also liberalization commitments on trade in services, investment and public procurement. The TPP also establishes rules on various subjects that are either only partially or not yet governed by World Trade Organization agreements. These include e-commerce, State-owned enterprises, regulatory coherence, the protection of intellectual property on the Internet and several labour and environmental issues. With this broad scope, the United States, which has been the main driver of this agreement, is seeking to set the "rules of the game" for the operation of value chains in the Asia-Pacific region in the coming decades (ECLAC, 2013a). It is estimated that the conclusion of the TPP could boost global income by US$ 295 billion and global exports by US$ 444 billion by 2025 (Petri, Plummer and Zhai, 2012).

The TPP contains a clause for the accession of new countries, which would allow the TPP to become a platform for the gradual creation of a free trade area of Asia and the Pacific —a project that has been under consideration by Asia-Pacific Economic Cooperation (APEC) since 2005. However, this would probably require achieving

convergence between the TPP and other large-scale economic integration projects that are currently under negotiation in the region. These include the Regional Comprehensive Economic Partnership, which involves Australia, China, India, Japan, New Zealand, the Republic of Korea and the 10 member countries of the Association of Southeast Asian Nations (ASEAN).

Once the TPP has undergone a legal review, it could be signed in early 2016, after which the agreement must be ratified by the parliaments of its member countries. Once it enters into force, the TPP will coexist with the many agreements that already exist among its members, such as the North American Free Trade Agreement (NAFTA) and several bilateral agreements signed by Chile, Mexico and Peru with Asian countries. Chile, in particular, already has existing trade agreements with all of the members of the TPP. Nevertheless, the information available indicates that the liberalization commitments negotiated in the TPP exceed those contained in several existing agreements and include, for example, greater liberalization of the agricultural sector in Canada and Japan. The three Latin American participants in the TPP are also members of the Pacific Alliance, while the fourth member of that Alliance, Colombia, has expressed interest in joining the TPP.

Source: Economic Commission for Latin America and the Caribbean (ECLAC), on the basis of ECLAC, *Latin America and the Caribbean in the World Economy 2013* (LC/G.2578-P), Santiago, 2013, chap. II; United States Trade Representative (USTR), "Summary of the Trans-Pacific Partnership Agreement" [online] https://ustr.gov/about-us/policy-offices/press-office/press-releases/2015/october/summary-trans-pacific-partnership; and Peter A. Petri, Michael G. Plummer and Fan Zhai, *The Trans-Pacific Partnership and Asia-Pacific Integration: A Quantitative Assessment*, Peterson Institute for International Economics, Washington, D.C., 2012.

In summary, the leading actors in the global economy are seeing domestic demand adjust downward and seeking to offset this lower demand by increasing exports. However, it is not possible for all to increase exports at a time when imports are declining in the system overall. This, then, is an insoluble equation or negative sum game in which each actor's efforts to achieve balance ultimately exacerbate its own imbalances and those of the system as a whole.

B. Latin America and the Caribbean records its worst export performance in eight decades

1. External trade will contract sharply in 2015

The weakness of aggregate global demand has negative implications for Latin America and the Caribbean, whose growth has historically been limited by external constraints that have led to stop-go situations and frequent currency and external debt crises. A production and export structure concentrated in low-productivity sectors and a lack of technological dynamism mean that the region's countries, notwithstanding their specificities, are highly vulnerable to the vagaries of international demand. This external constraint eased for several countries during the natural resource price boom but is operating strongly again now that the boom has ended. In other words, the export structure that characterizes the region is amplifying the negative effects of the drop in aggregate global demand. The persistence of current account imbalances and the lack of reciprocity in the relations between the major trade actors are additional factors in this vicious circle (see diagram I.1).

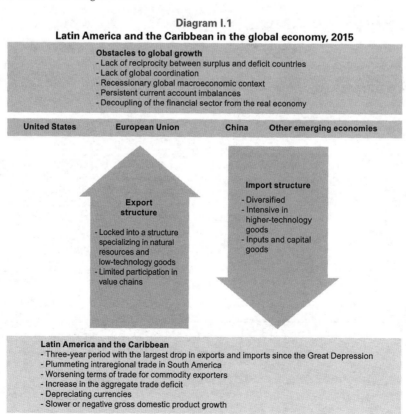

Diagram I.1
Latin America and the Caribbean in the global economy, 2015

Obstacles to global growth
- Lack of reciprocity between surplus and deficit countries
- Lack of global coordination
- Recessionary global macroeconomic context
- Persistent current account imbalances
- Decoupling of the financial sector from the real economy

United States   European Union   China   Other emerging economies

Export structure
- Locked into a structure specializing in natural resources and low-technology goods
- Limited participation in value chains

Import structure
- Diversified
- Intensive in higher-technology goods
- Inputs and capital goods

Latin America and the Caribbean
- Three-year period with the largest drop in exports and imports since the Great Depression
- Plummeting intraregional trade in South America
- Worsening terms of trade for commodity exporters
- Increase in the aggregate trade deficit
- Depreciating currencies
- Slower or negative gross domestic product growth

Source: Economic Commission for Latin America and the Caribbean (ECLAC).

The region's situation with production and exports, locked into an undiversified structure concentrated in natural resources and low-technology goods and with limited participation in international value chains, contrasts with its far more diversified import structure, in which higher-technology goods are strongly represented, especially intermediate inputs and capital goods essential to the functioning of the production and investment apparatus. External trade crises thus necessarily translate into slow growth and lower gross capital formation.

In the short run, the export production structure is constraining the region's ability to respond to price signals generated by the nominal depreciations affecting the currencies of many of its countries in recent months. From a medium-term perspective, its heavy dependence on raw material exports is an impediment to the structural shift towards more technology- and knowledge-intensive goods and services that is needed.

Notwithstanding the foregoing, it is worth noting that the challenges facing the Central American countries and Mexico are different from those of the commodity-exporting South American countries. Countries in the first group have been relatively successful in joining international production networks in manufacturing, in particular those related to the United States market. Thus, the major challenges for these countries are to move towards the export of higher-technology manufactured products with greater domestic value added and to reduce their heavy reliance on the United States market (especially in the case of Mexico). Similarly, most Caribbean countries depend largely on services exports, especially tourism.

Latin America and the Caribbean is highly vulnerable in this global context. The global growth slowdown has reduced the demand for and prices of the raw materials exported by the region, mainly metals and oil (see figure I.21). At the same time, the weak eurozone recovery and the slowdown in China have negatively affected exports to those two markets. Lastly, low GDP growth in the region has led to a drastic contraction in intraregional trade, except in Central America.

All commodity prices have fallen sharply since 2011

Figure I.21
World prices for selected commodity groups, 2000-2015 [a]
(Indices, 2005=100)

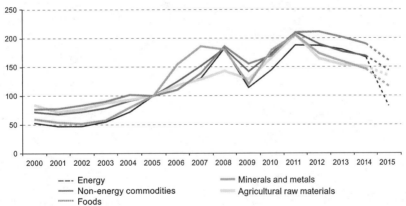

- - - Energy   ——— Minerals and metals
——— Non-energy commodities   ——— Agricultural raw materials
········· Foods

Source: Economic Commission for Latin America and the Caribbean (ECLAC), on the basis of figures from the World Bank, the International Monetary Fund (IMF) and The Economist Intelligence Unit (EIU).
[a] Figures for 2015 are projections.

During the decade-long commodities boom, the region —and especially South America— increased its dependence on exports of commodities, which dominate shipments to Asia and the European Union in particular. Commodities feature less strongly in exports to the region itself and the United States. Their smaller share of exports to this latter market is mainly explained by Mexican industrial exports: if Mexico is excluded, the share of commodities in the value of the region's exports to the United States in 2014 was 45% rather than 19% (see figure I.22).

The region has become even more dependent on commodity exports

Figure I.22
Latin America and the Caribbean: structure of exports to selected destinations by technology intensity, 2000, 2005 and 2014

(Percentages)

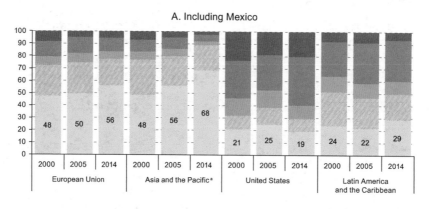

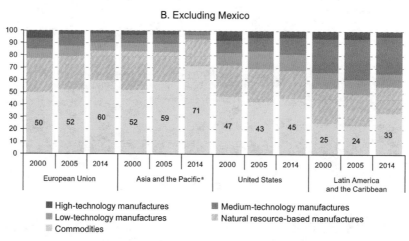

- High-technology manufactures
- Medium-technology manufactures
- Low-technology manufactures
- Natural resource-based manufactures
- Commodities

Source: Economic Commission for Latin America and the Caribbean (ECLAC), on the basis of the United Nations Commodity Trade Statistics Database (COMTRADE).
[a] Includes members of the Association of Southeast Asian Nations (ASEAN), Australia, China, India, Japan, New Zealand and the Republic of Korea.

In these circumstances, the Economic Commission for Latin America and the Caribbean (ECLAC) projects that the value of goods exports from the region to the world will drop by 14% in 2015, which will make three consecutive years of increasing declines in the value exported, turning 2013-2015 into the worst three-year period for the region's exports since 1931-1933, in the middle of the Great Depression. The contraction of the region's exports in 2015 will be mainly accounted for by a sharp drop in prices (-15%) that may not be offset by an expected small increase (1%) in volumes (see figure I.23 in annex I.A1). Meanwhile, the region's goods imports are projected to drop 10% by value as prices fall by 8.5% and volumes by 1.5% —once again, the third consecutive year of increasing declines (see figure I.24).

**The value of Latin American and Caribbean exports
to the world is projected to fall by 14% in 2015**

Figure I.23
Latin America and the Caribbean: annual variations in goods exports, 2000-2015 [a]
(Percentages)

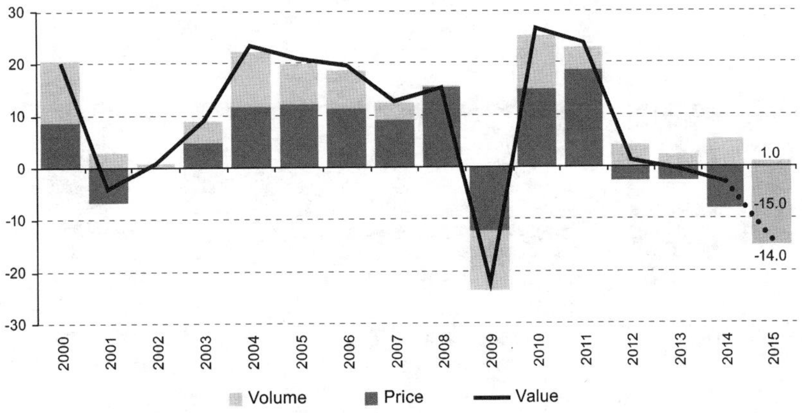

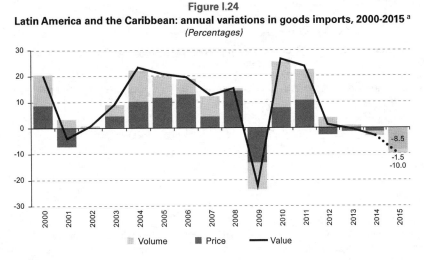

Source: Economic Commission for Latin America and the Caribbean (ECLAC), on the basis of official figures from the countries' central banks, customs offices and
national institutes of statistics.
[a] Figures for 2015 are projections.

The value of Latin American and Caribbean imports is projected to contract by 10% in 2015

Figure I.24
Latin America and the Caribbean: annual variations in goods imports, 2000-2015 [a]
(Percentages)

Source: Economic Commission for Latin America and the Caribbean (ECLAC), on the basis of official figures from the countries' central banks, customs offices and
national institutes of statistics.
[a] Figures for 2015 are projections.

By subregion, the largest drops in export prices are recorded in South America and the Caribbean, owing to their heavy dependence on commodities.[3] In South America, lower prices will be accompanied by a slight drop in export volumes. This situation contrasts with that projected for Mexico and Central America, where the expected price falls are much smaller and should be partially offset by higher volumes, cushioning the decline in export values (see figure I.25).

---

3   The sharp fall in prices in the Caribbean is attributable to the fact that the largest economy in the subregion, Trinidad and Tobago, is a net exporter of natural gas, whose international price has declined markedly in 2015. By contrast, most other Caribbean economies are net importers of commodities.

**South American export prices are expected to fall by 21%,
with volumes also declining marginally**

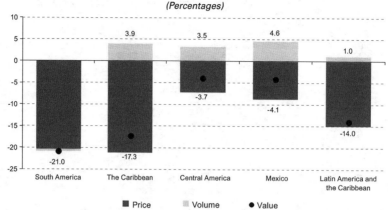

Figure I.25
**Latin America and the Caribbean (selected subregions and countries):
projected variations in exports by value, volume and price, 2015**
(Percentages)

Source: Economic Commission for Latin America and the Caribbean (ECLAC), on the basis of official figures from the countries' central banks, customs offices and national institutes of statistics.

The better performance projected for shipments from Mexico and Central America relative to South America is mainly accounted for by their differing export patterns. Whereas the United States absorbs 80% and 37% of the value of exports from Mexico and Central America, respectively, its share of South American exports exceeds 20% only in the cases of the Bolivarian Republic of Venezuela, Colombia, Ecuador, Guyana and Suriname. This makes a difference, as United States import demand has fallen less than European and Asian demand. Moreover, manufactures represent a larger share of the export baskets of Mexico and Central America than of South America overall. This has cushioned the decline in the value of exports, since prices for these goods (which make up 83% of the value of Mexico's exports) have not fallen as sharply as those for commodities.

Like exports, South America's imports will drop in price and volume in 2015. The main factor behind the first variable has been the large drop in the prices of imported fuels. As for the second, the most substantial declines have been in capital goods imports (machinery and intermediate inputs such as car parts, chemicals, tubing and metal products). Brazilian imports fell particularly sharply, declining 21% in value year-on-year between January and August. In the Caribbean, Central America and Mexico, conversely, import volumes are expected to increase, reflecting the greater dynamism of economic activity there than in South America (see figure I.26).

In 2015, the region's imports will decline in both price and volume

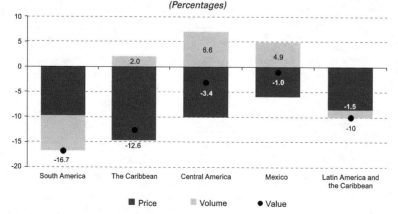

Figure I.26
**Latin America and the Caribbean (selected subregions and countries):
projected variations in imports by value, volume and price, 2015**
(Percentages)

Source: Economic Commission for Latin America and the Caribbean (ECLAC), on the basis of official figures from the countries' central banks, customs offices and national institutes of statistics.

By contrast with Brazil's, the value of Mexico's imports between January and August 2015 remained almost unchanged from the same period in 2014. The differing behaviour of imports in the region's two largest economies has been due to two factors. First, Mexico will register positive growth in 2015, whereas Brazilian GDP will contract sharply, depressing import demand. Second, their import structures are different. While Mexico largely imports intermediate goods that are incorporated into exports going essentially to the United States, which are forecast to grow 5% by volume in 2015, Brazil's imports are more closely tied to the recession of the local economy.

The decline in the region's exports and imports in 2015 will affect its trade with all its main partners. Besides the sharp contraction in intraregional trade (see subsection B.3), there will be a particularly large fall in trade with the European Union. The smallest decreases will be in exports to the United States, while in the case of imports, a slight increase is expected in those from Asia (see figure I.27 and annexes I.A2 and I.A3).

While South America, Mexico and Trinidad and Tobago will experience a negative terms-of-trade shock in 2015, the opposite may occur in Central America and the non-oil-producing countries of the Caribbean. The first group will be affected by lower prices for its main export products, such as hydrocarbons, minerals and metals and agricultural products. The second group, meanwhile, will benefit from the sharp drop in fuel prices (-40%), together with a 1% to 2% decline in food prices. Oil-exporting countries will experience the greatest deterioration in their terms of trade (see figure I.28 and map I.1). Meanwhile, the markets where the region's exports will undergo the greatest price declines are those that import mainly raw materials, such as China, the European Union and India (see map I.2).

In 2015, the region's trade with all its main partners will decline

Figure I.27
Latin America and the Caribbean: variations in the value of goods trade by origin and destination, 2014 and 2015 [a]
(Percentages)

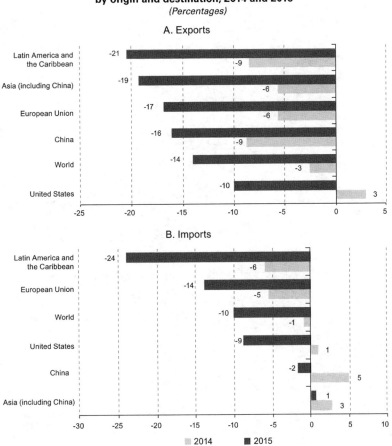

Source: Economic Commission for Latin America and the Caribbean (ECLAC), on the basis of official figures from the countries' central banks, customs offices and national institutes of statistics.
[a] Figures for 2015 are projections.

The terms of trade are worsening in the entire region except Central America and the non-oil-producing countries of the Caribbean

Figure I.28
Latin America and the Caribbean (selected groupings and countries): projected variations in the terms of trade, 2015
(Percentages)

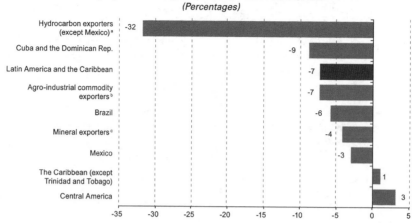

Source: Economic Commission for Latin America and the Caribbean (ECLAC), on the basis of official figures from the countries' central banks, customs offices and national institutes of statistics.
[a] The Bolivarian Republic of Venezuela, Colombia, Ecuador, the Plurinational State of Bolivia and Trinidad and Tobago.
[b] Argentina, Paraguay and Uruguay.
[c] Chile and Peru.

Oil-exporting countries have suffered the greatest price falls

Map I.1
Latin America and the Caribbean: projected average variations in export prices, 2015
(Percentages)

Source: Economic Commission for Latin America and the Caribbean (ECLAC), on the basis of the United Nations Commodity Trade Statistics Database (COMTRADE) and monthly price statistics from the World Bank, the Food and Agriculture Organization of the United Nations (FAO), the United Nations Conference on Trade and Development (UNCTAD) and the United States Departments of Commerce and Labor.
Note: The boundaries shown on this map do not imply official endorsement or acceptance by the United Nations.

Prices for the region's exports will fall most in China, India and Europe

Map I.2
Latin America and the Caribbean: projected average variations in export prices by destination country, 2015
(Percentages)

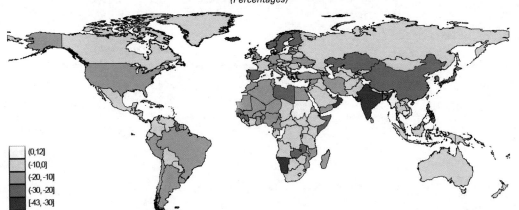

(0,12]
(-10,0]
(-20,-10]
(-30,-20]
[-43,-30]

Source: Economic Commission for Latin America and the Caribbean (ECLAC), on the basis of the United Nations Commodity Trade Statistics Database (COMTRADE) and monthly price statistics from the World Bank, the Food and Agriculture Organization of the United Nations (FAO), the United Nations Conference on Trade and Development (UNCTAD) and the United States Departments of Commerce and Labor.
Note: The boundaries shown on this map do not imply official endorsement or acceptance by the United Nations.

Exports from the countries of the Caribbean Community (CARICOM) are expected to fall by more than the regional average (-22%). This is due mainly to the drop in the natural gas price (-37%), which is expected to cause a 14% decline in the exports of the subregion's largest economy, Trinidad and Tobago. On the import side, a smaller drop of 13% is projected as lower prices (down by 15%) are partially offset by a 2% rise in volume. The performance of exports from the Dominican Republic is expected to be less negative than that of the CARICOM countries, with large price falls (especially for sugar), but an uptick in export volumes. The value of exports from Cuba is projected to drop by 13%, mainly because of sharp declines for oil (48%), ferronickel (30%) and sugar (27%) not fully offset by a larger volume of exports (see table I.1).

Higher export volumes are not offsetting large price falls

Table I.1
Latin America and the Caribbean: projected variations in foreign trade by country grouping and by value, volume and price, 2015
(Percentages)

Region, subregion or country	Exports			Imports		
	Price [a]	Volume	Value	Price [a]	Volume	Value
Latin America and the Caribbean	**-15.0**	**1.0**	**-14.0**	**-8.5**	**-1.5**	**-10.0**
Latin America	**-14.9**	**1.1**	**-13.8**	**-8.4**	**-1.4**	**-9.8**
South America	**-20.4**	**-0.6**	**-21.0**	**-9.7**	**-7.0**	**-16.7**
Southern Common Market (MERCOSUR)	**-20.5**	**0.0**	**-20.5**	**-9.8**	**-8.9**	**-18.8**
Argentina	-17.0	0.1	-16.9	-9.3	-0.6	-9.9
Brazil	-16.1	1.0	-15.1	-10.9	-11.7	-22.6
Paraguay	-11.4	-2.6	-13.9	-8.5	-5.1	-13.6
Uruguay	-7.0	-4.5	-11.5	-9.5	-6.2	-15.7
Venezuela (Bolivarian Republic of)	-46.5	5.9	-40.6	-7.0	-8.2	-15.2
Andean Community	**-24.0**	**-0.6**	**-24.6**	**-8.9**	**-3.8**	**-12.8**
Bolivia (Plurinational State of)	-25.1	-4.5	-29.6	-7.2	-6.1	-13.3
Colombia	-28.9	-0.3	-29.2	-7.7	-6.1	-13.8
Ecuador	-28.5	4.0	-24.5	-12.0	-8.9	-20.9
Peru	-15.0	-1.3	-16.3	-9.4	3.9	-5.5
Chile	**-13.4**	**-3.4**	**-16.8**	**-10.7**	**-3.0**	**-13.7**

Table I.1 (concluded)

Region, subregion or country	Exports			Imports		
	Price [a]	Volume	Value	Price [a]	Volume	Value
Central America	**-7.2**	**3.5**	**-3.7**	**-10.0**	**6.6**	**-3.4**
Costa Rica	-6.6	-8.6	-15.2	-9.5	0.4	-9.1
El Salvador	-3.9	9.0	5.1	-9.4	9.3	-0.1
Honduras	-6.4	5.2	-1.2	-9.4	14.1	4.7
Guatemala	-9.6	13.2	3.6	-10.1	8.7	-1.4
Nicaragua	-5.9	2.8	-3.1	-11.0	9.3	-1.6
Panama	-13.2	-2.0	-15.2	-11.0	3.3	-7.7
Mexico	**-8.7**	**4.6**	**-4.1**	**-5.9**	**4.9**	**-1.0**
Dominican Republic	**-16.8**	**4.4**	**-12.4**	**-12.5**	**0.9**	**-11.6**
Cuba	**-28.2**	**15.3**	**-12.9**	**-21.0**	**-9.4**	**-30.4**
Caribbean Community (CARICOM)	**-20,4**	**-1,5**	**-21,9**	**-14,6**	**2,0**	**-12,6**

Source: Economic Commission for Latin America and the Caribbean (ECLAC), on the basis of official figures from the countries' central banks, customs offices and national institutes of statistics.
[a] Price indices calculated using 2014 as the base year.

2. Trade deficits will grow despite nominal currency depreciations

Slow growth and uncertainty in the global economy, global current account imbalances and the type of specialization of the region's countries will result in the latter's trade balances deteriorating, in accordance with the logic implicit in diagram I.1. These deficits have forced them to carry out macroeconomic adjustments, which have contributed in turn to the stagnation and uncertainty in the global economy. The deficits recorded in the region since mid-2014 are expected to continue to widen in 2015. Thus most of the region's countries will end 2015 with a negative trade balance. In the aggregate, this is projected to more than double from US$ 30 billion in 2014 to some US$ 68 billion, the equivalent of 1.2% of regional GDP. The trade surplus of oil-exporting countries (except Mexico) is expected to all but disappear. Mineral exporters' surpluses will also decline, although by less.

Once again, the region's two largest economies are in contrasting situations. While Mexico's trade deficit will expand as a percentage of GDP, the larger scale of the macroeconomic adjustment in Brazil has led to a sharp contraction in imports. This is projected to turn what was a small deficit in 2014 into a surplus of just over US$ 13.8 billion in 2015, equivalent to 0.7% of GDP (see figure I.29). Meanwhile, the trade deficits traditionally run by the countries of Central America and the Caribbean Community (except Trinidad and Tobago) are expected to decline by between 2 and 3 percentage points of GDP because of cheaper oil and food imports (see table I.2).

The region's trade deficit is expected to double in 2015 as a share of GDP

Figure I.29
Latin America and the Caribbean (selected groupings and countries): trade balances, 2014-2015 [a]
(Percentages of GDP)

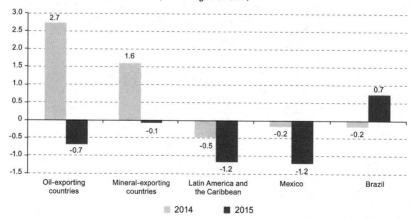

Source: Economic Commission for Latin America and the Caribbean (ECLAC), on the basis of official figures from the countries' central banks, customs offices and national institutes of statistics.
[a] Figures for 2015 are projections.

Only a few countries will run a trade surplus in 2015

Table I.2
Latin America and the Caribbean: trade balances, 2013-2015 [a]
(Millions of dollars and percentages of GDP)

Region, subregion or country	2013	2014	2015	2013	2014	2015
	Millions of dollars			Percentages of GDP		
Latin America and the Caribbean	**-3 781**	**-29 668**	**-67 860**	**-0.1**	**-0.5**	**-1.2**
Argentina	8 004	6 686	968	1.3	1.2	0.2
Bolivia (Plurinational State of)	2 319	1 731	-499	7.6	5.1	-1.3
Brazil	2 286	-3 959	13 718	0.1	-0.2	0.7
Chile	1 820	7 767	4 327	0.7	3.0	1.7
Colombia	3 180	-4 694	-12 864	0.8	-1.2	-4.0
Costa Rica	-5 748	-5 675	-5 716	-11.6	-11.4	-10.8
Cuba	70	582	1 889	0.1	0.7	2.2
Dominican Republic	-7 377	-7 369	-6 421	-12.1	-11.5	-9.8
Ecuador	-1 619	-1 135	-1 856	-1.7	-1.1	-1.7
El Salvador	-5 295	-5 208	-4 981	-21.8	-20.7	-19.2
Guatemala	-6 176	-6 058	-5 424	-11.5	-10.3	-8.7
Honduras	-3 147	-2 997	-3 615	-17.0	-15.5	-18.8
Mexico	-909	-2 111	-14 573	-0.1	-0.2	-1.2
Nicaragua	-2 333	-2 402	-2 418	-20.7	-20.3	-19.6
Panama (excluding Colón Free Zone)	-12 311	-12 880	-11 935	-28.9	-36.1	-31.5
Paraguay	2 303	1 817	1 531	8.0	5.9	5.1
Peru	-429	-404	-4 667	-0.2	-0.2	-2.4
Uruguay	-1 352	-918	-338	-2.4	-1.6	-0.6
Venezuela (Bolivarian Republic of)	30 900	16 937	-4 406	8.0	2.9	-0.6
Caribbean Community (CARICOM)	**-7 967**	**-9 378**	**-10 581**	**-11.4**	**-12.2**	**-13.1**
Trinidad and Tobago	3 899	2 902	389	16.0	9.5	1.2
Rest of CARICOM	**-11 866**	**-12 280**	**-10 970**	**-26.1**	**-26.7**	**-23.2**

Source: Economic Commission for Latin America and the Caribbean (ECLAC), on the basis of official figures from the countries' central banks, customs offices and national institutes of statistics.
[a] Figures for 2015 are projections.

Like other developing economies that are exporters of raw materials, a number of countries in the region have experienced large nominal currency depreciations since mid-2014. These depreciations have not stimulated exports as much as expected, for two reasons. First, a number of countries' exports are concentrated in a few products, which limits their ability to respond to the price signals generated by depreciations. Second, when several currencies depreciate simultaneously, the net effect is to reduce or even cancel out any competitiveness gains for each country (see figure I.30).

Simultaneous currency depreciations cancel out and do not boost exports

Figure I.30
Latin America (5 countries): monthly variations in nominal exchange-rate indices,
January 2000 to July 2015
(Indices, January 2000=100)

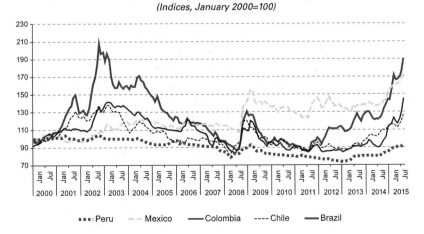

Source: Economic Commission for Latin America and the Caribbean (ECLAC), on the basis of official figures.

3. Intraregional trade has plummeted by even more than exports to the rest of the world

ECLAC projects that the value of intraregional exports will drop by about 21% in 2015, some 8 percentage points more than shipments to the rest of the world. This will be the second consecutive year's decline in shipments within the region, and also the second year in which they drop by more than extraregional exports (see figure I.31). Intraregional imports are expected to drop by even more than exports (-24%). This highlights the strongly procyclical behaviour of intraregional trade. The exception to this pattern is trade between Central American countries, as shown below.

Intraregional exports are falling by more than those to the rest of the world

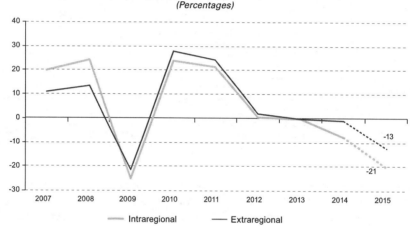

Figure I.31
Latin America and the Caribbean: variations in intraregional and extraregional exports by value, 2005-2015 [a]
(Percentages)

Source: Economic Commission for Latin America and the Caribbean (ECLAC), on the basis of official figures from the countries' central banks, customs offices and national institutes of statistics.
[a] Figures for 2015 are projections.

The largest declines in intraregional trade have been in South America and the Caribbean. In the first half of 2015, trade within MERCOSUR and within the Andean Community contracted by 23% and 20%, respectively. Trade between Argentina and Brazil contracted by 17% in the first half of 2015, with reciprocal purchases of industrial manufactures (especially intermediate goods, consumer durables and capital goods) falling yet more (25%).

The intraregional trade situation in South America stands in contrast to trade between the Central American countries, which grew slightly in the same period (see table I.3). In fact, whereas intraregional exports in South America are expected to drop by more than extraregional ones in 2015, the opposite is expected in Central America, where intraregional exports will expand slightly (see figure I.32). This is because of the greater dynamism of economic activity in the subregion and the greater depth of productive integration between its economies, which has been reinforced not only through Central American integration agreements, but also through trade agreements negotiated jointly by the Central American countries with their main trading partners outside the region (European Union, Mexico and the United States). Indeed, these three agreements allow for subregional cumulation of origin, thus promoting trade within Central American of inputs to be used in goods exported to these markets.

Intraregional trade plummeted in the first half of 2015

Table I.3
Latin America and the Caribbean (selected groupings and countries): variations in intraregional exports, first half of 2015 relative to the same period in 2014
(Percentages)

Origin / Destination	Southern Common Market (MERCOSUR)	Andean Community	Central American Common Market (CACM)	Caribbean Community (CARICOM)	Rest of Latin America and the Caribbean [a]	Latin America and the Caribbean
MERCOSUR	-23.0	-17.3	-20.2	-16.7	-9.5	-19.6
Andean Community	-34.1	-20.3	-44.8	-32.0	-32.8	-32.3
CACM	-16.7	15.6	0.4	-9.2	-3.9	-1.2
CARICOM	-20.7	-22.1	-22.1	-18.7	-22.1	-20.4
Chile	-19.5	-9.5	-10.7	-10.7	7.0	-12.6
Mexico	-5.8	-17.3	2.7	-11.3	-16.3	-8.7
Other countries of Latin America [b]	-16.1	-13.3	-13.5	-38.5	-13.4	-32.2
Latin America and the Caribbean	**-22.7**	**-17.1**	**-14.2**	**-21.2**	**-15.4**	**-19.3**

Source: Economic Commission for Latin America and the Caribbean (ECLAC), on the basis of official information from the countries and mirror statistics for the Caribbean countries, the Bolivarian Republic of Venezuela, Cuba and the Dominican Republic.
[a] Chile, Cuba, the Dominican Republic and Mexico.
[b] Aggregated data for Cuba and the Dominican Republic.

Intrasubregional trade is more countercyclical in Central America than in South America

Figure I.32
South America and Central America: variations in intraregional and extraregional exports by value, 2007-2015 [a]
(Percentages)

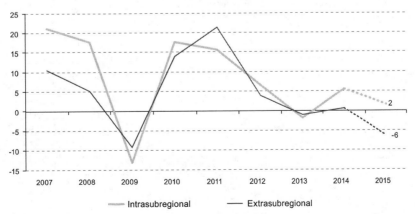

A. South America

B. Central America

— Intrasubregional — Extrasubregional

Source: Economic Commission for Latin America and the Caribbean (ECLAC), on the basis of official figures from the countries' central banks, customs offices and national institutes of statistics.
[a] Figures for 2015 are projections.

C. Conclusions

The factors that contributed to the outbreak of the crisis of 2008 and 2009 have persisted, so that the world economy has continued in a situation of low growth that is adversely affecting global and regional trade. For one thing, the powerful dynamic of the financial markets has been multiplying the instability associated with real imbalances between countries and excess saving in surplus economies. This, in turn, has led to the build-up of debt, financial fragility and fiscal austerity, depressing the level of activity. The effects of imbalances have fallen mainly on deficit countries, in the form of currency depreciation and lower growth. They have been felt most acutely in economies that are concentrated in a few products, where depreciation is less effective and the technological capabilities needed to react to the shifting structure of relative prices by increasing exportable output are lacking.

Macroeconomic policy is increasingly constrained in its ability to stimulate global economic activity. While monetary policy is hitting the limits of a zero or negative interest rate, fiscal policy is having to cope with barriers associated with the loss of fiscal space resulting from high levels of public debt or a reluctance to accept a larger role of the State in the economy. Failure to use all possible instruments to stimulate effective demand is reinforcing the deflationary tendencies of the current economic climate, even though many economies need large amounts of investment in infrastructure, the environment and new technologies.[4]

The weaknesses of global economic governance are a hindrance to coordinated expansion of global output and productive restructuring in deficit countries. This complex situation is being compounded by a mild slowdown in the Chinese economy and uncertainty about progress in rebalancing the country's development model, as well as slow European growth. Consequently, the global economic situation calls for greater macroeconomic policy coordination and more deleveraging of the financial system, which would help to reactivate aggregate demand and trade.

Meanwhile, a number of changes in the world trade dynamic account for some of its slowdown in the last decade, particularly the post-crisis period. The first is the combination of slow growth in the European Union and its large share of world trade. The weakness of European demand for imports has not been made up for by emerging economies such as Brazil, China and India, which account for much smaller shares of world imports. A second factor appears to be the mature stage now reached in the integration of China and eastern Europe into the global economy and trade, which may have reduced incentives to increase the geographical fragmentation of global production.

Third, the reduced share of investment goods and consumer durables in global demand since the crisis has exacerbated the trade slowdown, since these goods have a large imported component. Fourth, after a long process of accumulating production capabilities, China is increasingly substituting locally produced parts and components for imported ones, which is adversely affecting the global trade in intermediate goods.

In this context, 2015 will be the third consecutive year of increasing declines in Latin American and Caribbean exports by value. This has made the three-year period from 2013 to 2015 the region's worst in terms of export performance for eight decades. The large drop projected for the region's exports in terms of value reflects not just the weakness of demand from its main trading partners, but also the effects from the end of a commodity price cycle. The region's trade deficit will double as a proportion of output and the terms of trade of economies that are net exporters of commodities will worsen.

At the same time, the large drop in regional imports reflects the weakness of economic activity, especially in some of the larger economies. In particular, the sharp contraction of intraregional trade in South America is a serious matter because this kind of trade is the most conducive to production and export diversification.

Increasingly entrenched specialization in natural resources and the persistence of a structure dominated by low capacities will make it harder to escape today's difficult conditions. The fact that the boom associated with high commodity prices was not harnessed to develop new activities, goods and services will make it harder for the region to diversify its production and export structure today. Although this process could be stimulated by the nominal currency depreciations experienced by a number of its countries in recent months, the current concentration of the export basket sets limits to this.

---

[4] Eggertsson and Krugman (2012) show that, in situations where demand contracts as a result of the deleveraging of financial instruments by private agents, an expansionary fiscal policy can allow the economy to avoid unemployment and deflation.

The decline in currency earned from exports needs to be offset by greater capital inflows. This situation has increased the pressure to adjust public spending and real wages, which will hamper efforts to continue reducing poverty and inequality.

In this context, regional economic integration urgently needs to be deepened . A more integrated regional space with common rules is indispensable for promoting production linkages, enhancing the resilience of intraregional trade and fostering production and export diversification. Consequently, efforts to coordinate integration mechanisms and explore areas of convergence will have to be intensified. One of these areas is trade facilitation, an issue addressed in chapter III. It is also essential to deal with the region's shortcomings in terms of transport and telecommunications infrastructure in order to create an environment that is more propitious to the development of Latin American and Caribbean value chains. In parallel, the region should try to reap the maximum benefit from its increasing trade and economic ties with China, a subject addressed in the next chapter.

The current situation clearly shows that the region as a whole has not been able to add enough value to its natural resource exports, whether by processing them further, or incorporating technological advances with a view to diversifying them or generating new service exports associated with regional technical know-how in activities such as mining, agriculture and forestry. There is a major lack of industrial policy that must be corrected, since the incentive structure during the high commodity price period did not foster substantial private investment in this area.

Despite the difficulties of implementing industrial policies in a context of slow growth, the development of new export sectors is needed more than ever. In a crisis like the present one, strengthening industrial and technological policies in order to diversify, raise productivity and incorporate more knowledge into production is not only an economic imperative but also a fundamental factor in supporting employment and social stability.

Bibliography

Bernanke, B.S. (2005), "The Global Saving Glut and the U.S. Current Account Deficit", Homer Jones Lecture, St. Louis, Missouri, 14 April [online] http://www.federalreserve.gov/boarddocs/speeches/2005/200503102/.

Blanchard, Olivier (2015), "Looking forward, looking back", *IMF Survey Magazine*, 31 August [online] http://www.imf.org/external/pubs/ft/survey/so/2015/RES083115A.htm.

Constantinescu, Cristina, Aaditya Mattoo and Michele Ruta (2015), "The global trade slowdown: Cyclical or structural?", *IMF Working Paper*, No. WP/15/6, Washington, D.C., International Monetary Fund (IMF).

Cros, Daniel (2015), "Monetary policy and the over-investment cycle China as an extreme case", *CEPS Commentary*, Brussels [online] http://www.ceps.eu/system/files/DG%20Overinvestment%20cycle%20China.pdf .

ECLAC (Economic Commission for Latin America and the Caribbean) (2015), *Latin America and the Caribbean and China: Towards a new era in economic cooperation* (LC/L.4010), Santiago.

___ (2013a), *Latin America and the Caribbean in the World Economy 2013: A sluggish postcrisis, mega trade negotiations and value chains: scope for regional action, 2013* (LC/G.2578), Santiago.

___ (2013b), *Social Panorama of Latin America, 2013* (LC/G.2580), Santiago.

Eggertsson, Gauti B. and Paul Krugman, (2012), "Debt, deleveraging, and the liquidity trap: A Fisher-Minsky-Koo approach", *The Quarterly Journal of Economics*, vol. 127, No. 3, Oxford University Press.

EIU (The Economist Intelligence Unit) (2015), *World Commodity Forecasts: Industrial raw materials*, London, August.

European Commission (2015), *European Economic Forecast*, Brussels, Winter.

Fischer, Stanley (2015), "Monetary policy in the United States and in developing countries", speech at the Crockett Governors' Roundtable 2015 for African Central Bankers, University of Oxford, Oxford, 30 June [online] http://www.federalreserve.gov/newsevents/speech/fischer20150630a.htm.

Francis, Michael and Louis Morel (2015), "The slowdown in global trade", *Bank of Canada Review*, Ottawa, Spring.

Hoekman, B. (ed.) (2015), *The Global Trade Slowdown: A new normal*, A VoxEU E-book, London, CEPR.

IMF (International Monetary Fund) (2015), *2015 External Sector Report*, Washington, D.C., 27 July.

Kregel, J. (2014), "Liquidity preference and the entry and exit to ZIRP and QE", *Policy Note*, 2014-5, Levy Economics Institute of Bard College, Annandale-On-Hudson, NY.

Krugman, P. (2015), "A movable glut", *New York Times*, 24 August [online] http://www.nytimes.com/2015/08/24/opinion/a-moveable-glut.html?_r=0.

McKinsey Global Institute (2015), "Debt and (not much) deleveraging", London, February.

OECD (Organization for Economic Cooperation and Development) (2015a), *In it together: Why less inequality benefits all*, Paris, OECD Publishing.

___ (2015b), *Economic Survey of China*, Paris.

Petri, Peter A., Michael G. Plummer and Fan Zhai (2012), *The Trans-Pacific Partnership and Asia-Pacific Integration: A quantitative assessment*, Peterson Institute for International Economics, Washington, D.C.

Summers, Lawrence (2014), "U.S. economic prospects: Secular stagnation, hysteresis, and the zero lower bound", *Business Economics,* vol. 49, No. 2 [online] http://larrysummers.com/wp-content/uploads/2014/06/NABE-speech-Lawrence-H.-Summers1.pdf .

Veenendaal, Paul and others (2015), "A value-added trade perspective on recent patterns in world trade", *The Global Trade Slowdown: A new normal*, B. Hoekman (ed.), A VoxEU E-book, London, CEPR.

World Bank (2015a), *Commodity Markets Outlook*, Washington, D.C., July.

___ (2015b), *Global Economic Prospects*, Washington, D.C., January.

___ (2015c), "China Economic Update", Washington, D.C., June.

Annex I.A1

Latin America and the Caribbean: imports and exports, 2013-2015
(Millions of dollars)

Region, subregion or country	Exports			Imports		
	2013	2014	2015	2013	2014	2015
Latin America and the Caribbean [a]	**1 109 298**	**1 078 519**	**928 884**	**1 113 079**	**1 108 186**	**996 744**
Latin America	**1 088 691**	**1 059 596**	**914 318**	**1 086 919**	**1 082 414**	**974 011**
South America	**653 478**	**605 592**	**480 201**	**606 066**	**581 765**	**484 287**
Southern Common Market (MERCOSUR)	**436 517**	**394 532**	**315 175**	**394 376**	**373 969**	**303 701**
Argentina	81 660	71 935	59 758	73 656	65 249	58 790
Brazil	242 034	225 101	191 011	239 748	229 060	177 292
Paraguay	13 605	13 117	11 294	11 302	11 299	9 763
Uruguay	10 256	10 380	9 186	11 608	11 298	9 524
Venezuela (Bolivarian Republic of)	88 962	74 000	43 956	58 062	57 063	48 333
Andean Community	**140 484**	**135 385**	**102 154**	**137 033**	**139 887**	**121 981**
Bolivia (Plurinational State of)	11 657	12 266	8 635	9 338	10 535	9 134
Colombia	60 281	56 982	40 343	57 101	61 676	53 165
Ecuador	25 686	26 604	20 086	27 305	27 740	21 942
Peru	42 861	39 533	33 073	43 290	39 937	37 740
Chile	**76 477**	**75 675**	**62 962**	**74 657**	**67 908**	**58 605**
Central America	**35 338**	**36 902**	**34 506**	**70 227**	**72 137**	**69 918**
Costa Rica	8 879	9 139	7 750	14 627	14 814	13 466
El Salvador	4 334	4 256	4 473	9 629	9 463	9 454
Guatemala	10 183	10 994	11 389	16 359	17 052	16 813
Honduras	7 805	8 072	7 975	10 953	11 070	11 590
Nicaragua	3 292	3 622	3 510	5 624	6 024	5 686
Panama	17 160	15 332	11 867	24 136	23 479	22 094
Panama (excluding Colón Free Zone)	812	689	584	13 123	13 569	12 519
Mexico	**380 729**	**397 866**	**381 554**	**381 638**	**399 977**	**395 977**
The Caribbean	**39 786**	**38 288**	**31 698**	**55 060**	**54 453**	**47 274**
Caribbean Community (CARICOM)	**21 522**	**19 877**	**15 614**	**29 489**	**29 255**	**26 096**
Bahamas	955	849	694	3 166	3 270	2 783
Barbados	458	474	406	1 681	1 652	1 488
Belize	608	589	587	876	926	693
Guyana	1 376	1 167	997	1 847	1 779	1 573
Haiti	915	954	949	3 329	3 483	3 362
Jamaica	1 580	1 453	1 050	5 462	5 184	4 491
Suriname	2 395	2 149	1 942	2 126	1 966	1 756
Trinidad and Tobago	12 770	11 806	8 618	8 871	8 904	8 129
Organization of Eastern Caribbean States (OECS)	**465**	**436**	**371**	**2 131**	**2 091**	**1 820**
Antigua and Barbuda	68	55	51	503	500	454
Dominica	41	41	37	179	181	177
Grenada	45	46	49	324	299	290
Saint Kitts and Nevis	57	58	56	252	270	253
Saint Lucia	200	182	125	546	522	339
Saint Vincent and the Grenadines	54	54	54	327	319	308
Cuba	**8 840**	**8 492**	**7 395**	**8 770**	**7 910**	**5 898**
Dominican Republic	**9 424**	**9 920**	**8 689**	**16 801**	**17 288**	**15 280**

Source: Economic Commission for Latin America and the Caribbean (ECLAC), on the basis of official information from the countries on their balance of payments to 2014 and estimates for 2015, based on monthly information from central banks and statistics bureaux for the period from January to August or September, depending on the information available in each country. In the case of the Caribbean Community (CARICOM) countries and Panama, which includes the Colón Free Zone, the estimates for 2015 assume the trade product structure given by the United Nations Commodity Trade Statistics Database (COMTRADE) and only consider price changes, with no variation in volumes, since full monthly information was not available from the countries for 2015. In the cases of the Bolivarian Republic of Venezuela, Cuba and the Dominican Republic, the projections for 2015 are based on mirror data from their trading partners.
[a] Excludes re-exports from the Colón Free Zone.

Annex I.A2

**Latin America and the Caribbean: variations in exports
to selected destinations by value, 2014 and 2015**
(Percentages)

Region, subregion or country	European Union		United States		China		Rest of Asia		Latin America and the Caribbean	
	2014	2015	2014	2015	2014	2015	2014	2015	2014	2015
Latin America and the Caribbean	**-6.2**	**-17.3**	**3.2**	**-9.8**	**-8.8**	**-16.2**	**-1.8**	**-21.6**	**-7.6**	**-20.5**
Argentina	-3.7	-14.6	-12.3	-11.0	-27.4	-7.2	-4.1	2.5	-13.9	-26.9
Bolivia (Plurinational State of)	-7.3	-2.1	65.9	-41.8	36.7	0.8	28.8	-13.1	-4.2	-33.5
Brazil	-12.0	-17.5	9.6	-12.7	-11.8	-7.2	4.0	-19.0	-14.9	-22.2
Chile	-2.5	-21.0	-4.7	-6.6	-3.4	-10.3	5.8	-20.1	-2.3	-20.6
Colombia	-0.7	-24.7	-24.0	-26.5	10.1	-62.2	8.5	9.4	-11.6	-19.3
Costa Rica	-3.2	-10.2	-4.1	-10.7	-9.0	-76.7	-10.4	-73.9	4.9	0.7
Ecuador	-2.1	-5.6	1.4	-26.9	-11.8	55.8	30.2	-3.6	-6.0	-34.3
El Salvador	22.7	1.9	-1.8	5.0	-87.7	639.3	5.1	6.7	-1.2	3.2
Guatemala	21.9	11.7	2.0	-0.8	-74.5	316.0	29.3	-10.3	8.2	2.8
Honduras	6.8	11.4	3.4	-2.1	-47.2	-77.7	9.7	-28.2	7.3	2.1
Mexico	3.0	-8.5	6.3	-3.5	-7.8	-19.9	-2.4	-5.1	-7.5	-7.3
Nicaragua	-13.6	15.4	34.6	15.8	0.0	0.0	7.0	-3.2	10.2	-5.6
Panama [a]	24.6	-30.0	3.0	-28.5	35.0	-43.1	-22.7	21.1	-12.7	3.9
Paraguay	-1.7	-7.3	-17.2	-23.2	-16.0	-30.3	33.0	-49.8	1.4	-6.9
Peru	-6.8	-19.2	-16.7	-25.8	-5.0	-1.9	-25.5	-19.4	1.2	-25.7
Uruguay	-5.7	-14.2	18.8	26.1	-5.5	-8.7	12.7	-21.2	-3.1	-25.7
Venezuela (Bolivarian Republic of)	-0.6	-55.2	-3.3	-43.9	-7.2	-50.7	-16.0	-50.6	-2.6	-33.6
Caribbean Community (CARICOM)	-12.4	-15.1	-16.0	-15.3	22.0	-25.0	-50.5	-35.8	-10.2	-29.8

Source: Economic Commission for Latin America and the Caribbean (ECLAC), on the basis of official figures from the countries' central banks, customs offices and national institutes of statistics.
[a] Excludes re-exports from the Colón Free Trade Zone.

Annex I.A3

Latin America and the Caribbean: variations in imports from selected origins by value, 2014 and 2015
(Percentages)

Region, subregion or country	European Union		United States		China		Rest of Asia		Latin America and the Caribbean	
	2014	2015	2014	2015	2014	2015	2014	2015	2014	2015
Latin America and the Caribbean	**-6.2**	**-13.5**	**2.6**	**-8.5**	**4.5**	**-1.5**	**-0.5**	**3.5**	**-5.9**	**-23.9**
Argentina	-15.2	-12.5	10.4	-10.5	-5.3	3.4	-14.8	-1.4	-21.3	-26.4
Bolivia (Plurinational State of)	7.0	-20.5	6.1	-14.7	45.3	-10.7	21.4	-16.1	3.8	-9.2
Brazil	-8.0	-18.4	-2.8	-21.9	0.1	-14.8	-5.8	-18.0	-7.9	-32.3
Chile	-20.1	-11.2	-11.3	-16.6	-3.6	-3.2	-6.6	-5.1	-5.3	-20.0
Colombia	9.9	-3.3	11.6	-11.5	13.8	-16.1	3.2	-13.2	-5.0	-21.7
Costa Rica	5.4	5.8	1.9	-12.4	11.1	2.5	2.1	2.4	5.9	-13.7
Ecuador	3.1	-15.6	11.0	-33.0	4.7	-12.2	-1.9	-6.7	-2.0	-21.5
El Salvador	-10.2	5.7	2.9	-3.7	125.4	-100.0	0.8	-0.2	-5.8	-4.1
Guatemala	-4.1	-3.5	21.6	-7.8	35.7	8.2	6.3	4.0	-2.4	1.1
Honduras	35.0	15.5	0.7	-15.0	55.7	92.4	20.1	45.4	-9.5	0.4
Mexico	3.3	-13.2	4.3	-2.8	8.0	5.3	5.6	7.3	0.8	-17.4
Nicaragua	-11.4	38.4	0.9	22.1	...	...	22.2	-3.3	-3.1	-17.5
Panama	-21.6	-5.9	8.5	-3.9	8.8	0.5	4.2	8.2	-16.2	0.3
Paraguay	3.2	-8.0	21.6	-16.8	-10.4	-21.0	29.0	36.9	6.2	-18.8
Peru	-10.0	-5.8	-5.2	-3.3	0.2	-0.2	-12.6	9.8	-8.4	-13.7
Uruguay	7.6	8.7	7.2	-18.7	8.0	-17.0	-4.7	0.3	-1.8	-22.0
Venezuela (Bolivarian Republic of)	-18.9	-38.9	-12.0	-23.9	10.4	35.6	-30.2	560.9	-3.1	-47.7
Caribbean Community (CARICOM)	-15.3	-5.5	-30.1	-9.4	42.2	-4.3	6.1	-15.1	8.7	-28.1

Source: Economic Commission for Latin America and the Caribbean (ECLAC), on the basis of official figures from the countries' central banks, customs offices and national institutes of statistics.

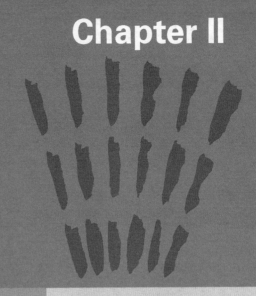

Chapter II

Opportunities to diversify trade and strengthen linkages with China

Introduction

China continues to gain stature in the global economy and trade, as well as in global value chains. Between 2000 and 2014, China accounted for 22% of growth in global gross domestic product (GDP) and 14% of growth in global exports of goods and services. Between 2007 and 2014 these figures were even higher, at 33% and 20%, respectively. Furthermore, China became the world's largest economy in 2014, measured by purchasing power parity.

The countries of Latin America and the Caribbean seized upon this source of growth in global demand. From 1% of Latin America's exports in 2000, China came to absorb 10% in 2014, while imports from China increased from 2% to 17% of total imports into the region, with which China overtook the European Union as the region's second largest trade partner.

Notwithstanding its rapid expansion, trade between Latin America and the Caribbean and China presents several shortcomings. Regional exports to China are highly concentrated in a small number of countries, products and companies, and consist mainly of primary products. This has led to a reprimarization of regional exports, high environmental costs, the concentration of exports in the hands of a few economic agents and an accelerated pace of deindustrialization. Positive spillover effects, including the spread of technology and knowledge, have also failed to materialize, owing to the interindustrial nature of trade.

This chapter addresses the structure of trade, foreign direct investment (FDI) and production linkages between the region and China, and examines the opportunities available to diversify these flows.

A. Changes in China will continue to affect regional trade

China's current development strategy seeks to shift the engine of growth from investment and exports to private consumption, by increasing disposable income. It also aims to further diversify the production of knowledge-intensive industries, develop services, progress toward cleaner production and increase innovation. These goals are likely to be reinforced by the five-year plan from 2016 to 2020.

China's less investment-intensive development pattern is already affecting Latin America through its construction sector's lower demand for raw materials such as copper and iron. This has heavily impacted countries that export these metals, such as Brazil, Chile and Peru. Exporters of other commodities —such as agricultural products— bought by sectors of the Chinese economy that have slowed less, have been less affected.

The Government of China continues to promote rapid urbanization under the new economic model. The New Type of Urbanization Plan 2014-2020 envisages a rise in the urban population from 54% to 60% of the total by 2020, which would mean 66 million people leaving the countryside for the city. China also has a rapidly expanding middle class,[1] which is changing its food consumption patterns, as higher urban incomes are associated with a dietary shift towards protein, processed foods and higher-quality and specialist food in general (United States Grains Council, 2011).

Rising consumption and urbanization could benefit food-producing countries in Latin America and the Caribbean. Over the coming decades, China is expected to sharply increase its imports of a wide range of raw and processed food products, such as palm oil, sugar, meat, dairy, processed and unprocessed cereals, fruit, coffee and legumes.

---

[1]   China's middle class (defined as those whose households spend between US$ 10 and US$ 100 a day on average) will represent 44% of the population by 2020 (607 million people), compared with 18% in 2012, according to economist Homi Kharas (*The Wall Street Journal*, 2012).

In the manufacturing industry, restructuring focuses on the transition towards strategic emerging industries. The Made in China 2025 plan seeks to increase computerization and promote the development of digital networks and the upgrading of traditional industries. The Internet Plus programme aims to increase the use of mobile Internet, cloud computing, big data and the Internet of Things in the manufacturing industry. Sectoral restructuring is being undertaken to improve energy efficiency and reduce emissions, transforming industries associated with energy conservation and environmental protection into new engines of growth and employment.

China has also launched a number of initiatives aimed at strengthening economic ties with its surrounding regions. These include the infrastructure mega-project known as the "Silk Road Economic Belt" and the creation of the Asian Infrastructure Investment Bank (see box II.1). China has also recently concluded free trade agreements (FTAs) with Australia and the Republic of Korea; it is currently negotiating a trilateral FTA with the latter country and Japan; and it is actively promoting the Regional Comprehensive Economic Partnership (RCEP) project. This will create a large free trade area encompassing Australia, China, India, Japan, New Zealand, the Republic of Korea and the 10 member countries of the Association of Southeast Asian Nations (ASEAN) (ECLAC, 2015a).

Box II.1
The Silk Road and the new development banks

The Silk Road Economic Belt and Twenty-first Century Maritime Silk Road Initiative was formalized in March 2015. Its aim is to strengthen economic ties between China, the rest of Asia, the Middle East, Africa and Europe, by developing a number of economic corridors over both land and sea. A further aim is to promote economic development in the different participating countries and regions. For example, the Silk Road Economic Belt aims to promote the development of the inland regions of China (which are less advanced than the coastal regions) and of the countries of Central Asia, by improving their connectivity with Asia-Pacific and European markets. The Chinese authorities estimate that the various projects encompassed by this initiative will impact a population of 4.4 billion people in 65 countries, and that, as a result, trade between China and the other participating countries could reach US$ 2.5 trillion in a decade.

Two international financial institutions proposed by the Chinese government are in the process of being established.

The Asian Infrastructure Investment Bank (AIIB, announced in October 2013 and formalized on 20 June 2015) aims to promote interconnectivity and economic integration in Asia by providing support to projects concerning energy, transportation, telecommunications, agricultural development, access to drinking water, irrigation, environmental protection and logistics. AIIB is envisaged as a multilateral development bank that will cooperate with other similar institutions existing in Asia, particularly the Asian Development Bank. Its membership includes 57 countries, of which nearly 40% are non-Asian, including a large bloc of European countries. Brazil is the only Latin American member. The New Development Bank (NDB), which was established in July 2014 and was previously known as the BRICS Development Bank, is another multilateral development bank whose members are Brazil, the Russian Federation, India, China and South Africa. It has a starting capital of US$ 100 billion.

Source: Economic Commission for Latin America and the Caribbean (ECLAC), *Latin America and the Caribbean and China: Towards a new era in economic cooperation* (LC/L.4010), Santiago, May 2015.

B. Asymmetry is increasing in trade, investment and value chain integration

1. Exports to China and its investment in the region are concentrated in primary goods and related products

Following strong growth in the value of regional goods trade with China between 2000 and 2011, bilateral trade has lost momentum. Between 2011 and 2015, growth of export value first slowed, with some fluctuations, then fell outright in 2014 and early 2015, owing to lower prices and demand for the main export products (see figure II.1 and chapter I). As the value of imports from China to Latin America and the Caribbean continued to rise in 2014, the region's trade deficit with China widened, reaching almost 80% of the value of the region's exports to that destination. Mexico accounted for 85% of this deficit.

Figure II.1
**Latin America and the Caribbean: value of exports, imports
and trade balance with China, 2000-2015**

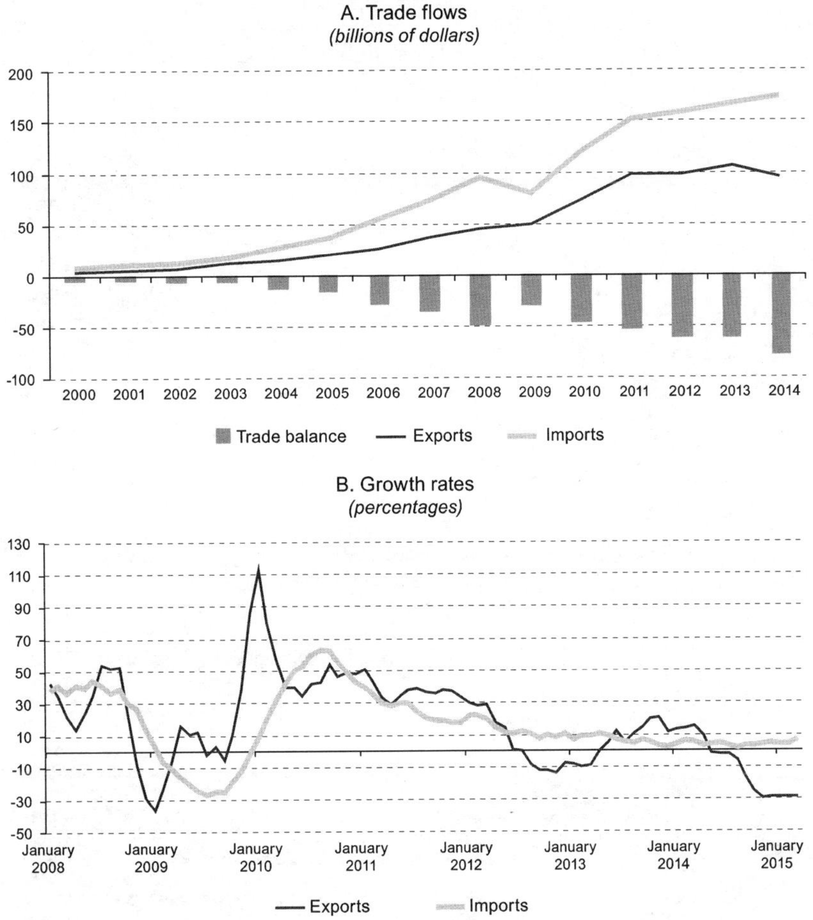

A. Trade flows
(billions of dollars)

■ Trade balance — Exports ▬ Imports

B. Growth rates
(percentages)

— Exports ▬ Imports

Source: Economic Commission for Latin America and the Caribbean (ECLAC), on the basis of information from the United Nations Commodity Trade Statistics Database (COMTRADE), and data from the National Bureau of Statistics of China.

The growth of the region's trade deficit with China is due mainly to trade in medium- and high-technology manufactures. Trade deficits are growing in particular in machinery and equipment and, to a lesser extent, in intermediate and consumer goods, and are only partly offset by a growing surplus on the primary goods balance (see figure II.2).[2]

With the exception of Central America, the subregions of Latin America and the Caribbean have seen their exports to China increasingly concentrated in primary goods (see figure II.3). In South America these goods (particularly agricultural products, iron ore, non-ferrous ore and crude oil) accounted for almost 75% of the total export value in 2013, and they made up 60% in the Caribbean countries (particularly non-ferrous ore). Mexico, with its more diverse export basket, also showed a sharp rise in the share of primary goods in exports (primarily non-ferrous ore, followed by iron ore and crude oil), reaching 45% in 2013. However, the share of consumer goods exports (mostly automobiles and motorcycles) from Mexico also rose significantly, to 20% in 2013, while the share of machinery and equipment and, to a lesser extent, intermediate goods dropped significantly.

---

[2]   The classification of goods is taken from *Comptes Harmonisés sur les* Échanges *et l'*Économie Mondiale (CHELEM) of the Centre d'Études Prospectives et d'Informations Internationales (CEPII), which is based on the production stage of the goods. The intermediate goods group also includes basic manufactures.

Figure II.2
Latin America and the Caribbean: trade balances with China
by type of good, 2000, 2005, 2010 and 2013
(Billions of dollars)

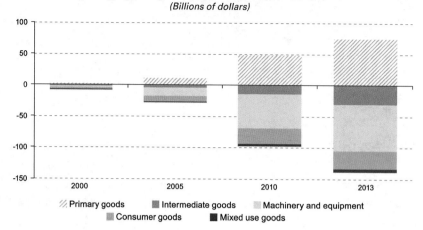

Source: Economic Commission for Latin America and the Caribbean (ECLAC), on the basis of information from Centre d'Études Prospectives et d'Informations Internationales (CEPII), *Trade Flows Characterization* database.

Figure II.3
Latin America and the Caribbean: structure of exports to China
by type of good, 2000, 2005 and 2013
(Percentages)

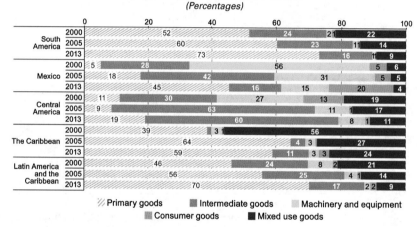

Source: Economic Commission for Latin America and the Caribbean (ECLAC), on the basis of information from Centre d'Études Prospectives et d'Informations Internationales (CEPII), *Trade Flows Characterization* database.

Central American exports are largely concentrated in intermediate goods (60% in 2013), mostly electronic components that, until 2014, were produced in Costa Rica for the Chinese market. Apart from primary goods, the share of the other categories —machinery and equipment in particular— have fallen since 2000.

In all the goods categories examined, exports from the region to China are largely accounted for by just a few countries (see figure II.4). Brazil is the largest exporter of primary and mixed use goods and the second largest in the other three categories. However, Brazilian exports to China (43% of the regional total in 2013) are concentrated in primary goods (particularly agricultural products and iron ore), which represented over 80% of the total export value in 2013. Chile is the main exporter of intermediate goods (particularly non-ferrous metals, largely copper, with around 50% of total Chilean exports), while Mexico is responsible for the bulk of consumer goods and machinery and equipment exports. However, despite being an important destination for Brazilian and Chilean exports (19% and 24%, respectively, in 2013), China has only a small share in exports from Mexico (2%).

Figure II.4
**Latin America and the Caribbean: structure of exports to China
by country of origin and type of good, 2013**
(Percentages)

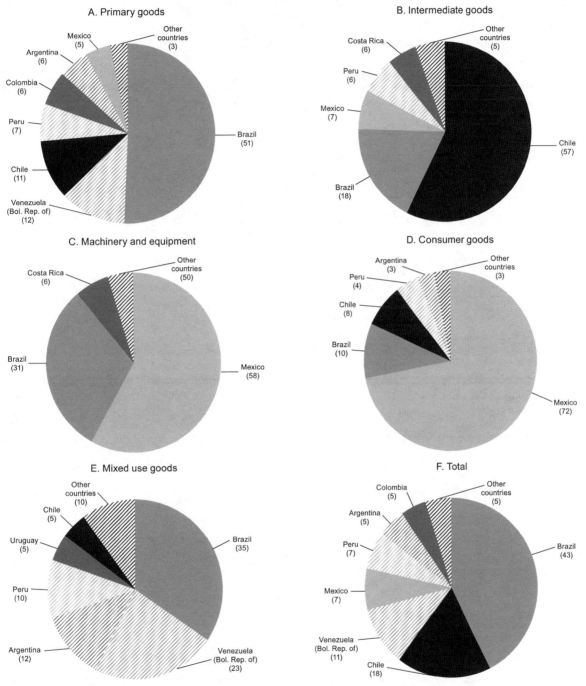

A. Primary goods

Other countries (3)
Mexico (5)
Argentina (6)
Colombia (6)
Peru (7)
Chile (11)
Venezuela (Bol. Rep. of) (12)
Brazil (51)

B. Intermediate goods

Other countries (5)
Costa Rica (6)
Peru (6)
Mexico (7)
Brazil (18)
Chile (57)

C. Machinery and equipment

Other countries (50)
Costa Rica (6)
Brazil (31)
Mexico (58)

D. Consumer goods

Argentina (3)
Other countries (3)
Peru (4)
Chile (8)
Brazil (10)
Mexico (72)

E. Mixed use goods

Other countries (10)
Chile (5)
Uruguay (5)
Peru (10)
Argentina (12)
Brazil (35)
Venezuela (Bol. Rep. of) (23)

F. Total

Colombia (5)
Argentina (5)
Other countries (5)
Peru (7)
Mexico (7)
Venezuela (Bol. Rep. of) (11)
Chile (18)
Brazil (43)

Source: Economic Commission for Latin America and the Caribbean (ECLAC), on the basis of information from Centre d'Etudes Prospectives et d'Informations Internationales (CEPII), *Trade Flows Characterization* database.

For China, Latin America and the Caribbean is an important supplier of primary goods imports (accounting for 15% of these imports in 2013) and, to a lesser extent, of mixed use goods (7%) (see figure II.5).[3] Conversely, the region provides only a very small proportion of China's imports of goods from other categories, particularly the more sophisticated goods. Apart from primary goods, the main origin of Chinese imports is the rest of Asia itself.

Figure II.5
China: structure of goods imports by region of origin, 2013
(Percentages)

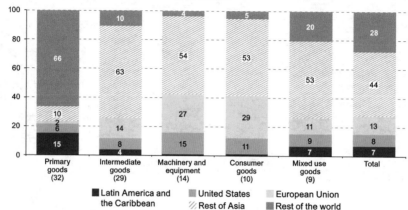

Source: Economic Commission for Latin America and the Caribbean (ECLAC), on the basis of information from Centre d'Etudes Prospectives et d'Informations Internationales (CEPII), *Trade Flows Characterization* database.

Note: Percentages in brackets next to the name of each category correspond to the share in the total value of China's imports in 2013. The "unclassified" category has not been included but accounts for 6% of that year's total.

The number of products the region exports to China has risen since 2000, but remains very low in comparison with its exports to the United States, the European Union and other countries within the region. In 2014, most of the Latin American countries exported between 1,000 and 4,000 products to the regional market, but none exported more than 400 to China except Brazil and Mexico, which exported around 1,400 (see figure II.6).

Figure II.6
Latin America and the Caribbean (selected countries): number of products exported to China, 2000-2014 [a]

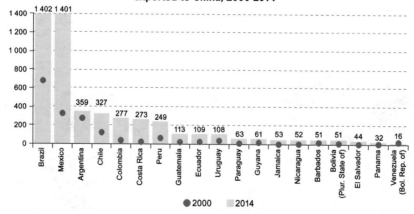

Source: Economic Commission for Latin America and the Caribbean (ECLAC), on the basis of information from the United Nations Commodity Trade Statistics Database (COMTRADE).

[a] At the six-digit level of the Harmonized Commodity Description and Coding System.

---

[3] Brazil and Argentina were the largest and third largest suppliers of agricultural products. Brazil was also China's second largest supplier of iron ore, after Australia. Chile was the main provider of non-ferrous metal, with its copper exports.

The region's exports to China are becoming increasingly concentrated in a small number of products within an already limited export basket. The 10 main export products, mostly commodities, accounted for 71% of the total export value to China in 2014, compared with 50% in 2003 (see figure II.7). By contrast, the 10 main products, mostly electronics, accounted for only 13% of the total value imported from China that year.

Figure II.7
Latin America and the Caribbean: top 10 products exported to China, 2000-2014
(Percentages of total exports to China)

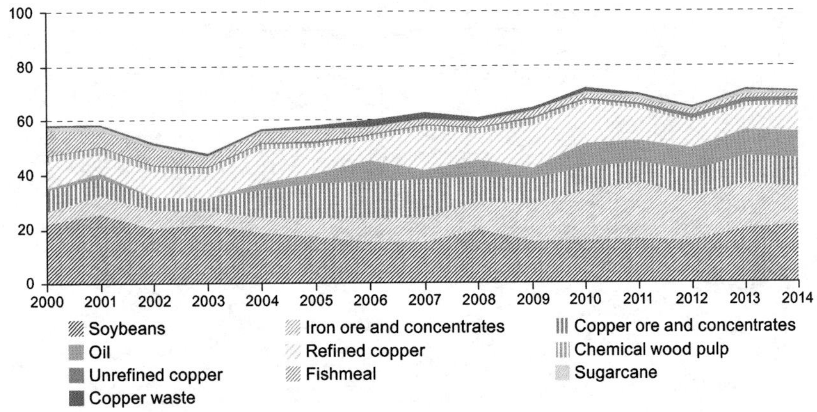

Soybeans	Iron ore and concentrates	Copper ore and concentrates
Oil	Refined copper	Chemical wood pulp
Unrefined copper	Fishmeal	Sugarcane
Copper waste		

Source: Economic Commission for Latin America and the Caribbean (ECLAC), on the basis of information from the United Nations Commodity Trade Statistics Database (COMTRADE).

2. The structure of the export business to China is highly concentrated

The region's exports to China are also concentrated in a handful of companies. In a study of eight countries, the five leading export companies accounted for an average of 33.4% of the respective country's total worldwide exports in 2011. However, the figure was much higher for exports to China (57%) (see table II.1). Small and medium-sized enterprises (SMEs) comprise the majority of export companies (89.4%), but account for only 8.8% of global exports.[4] Both figures are smaller for SME exports to China: 79.9% and 5.6%, respectively.

Table II.1
Latin America (8 countries): export company indicators, 2011
(Percentages)

		Worldwide	To China
Concentration of export value	Five main companies	33.4	57.4
	10 main companies	41.3	62.8
SME share [a]	In the total number of exporters	89.4	79.9
	In total export value	8.8	5.6

Source: Economic Commission for Latin America and the Caribbean (ECLAC), on the basis of figures provided by the national customs offices of eight countries (Chile, Costa Rica, Ecuador, El Salvador, Guatemala, Peru, Plurinational State of Bolivia and Uruguay).
[a] Export SMEs are defined as firms exporting amounts of less than the respective country's per capita GDP, expressed in purchasing power parity (PPP), multiplied by 1,000.

The number of Latin American exporters shipping to China grew significantly between 2007 and 2011: by 7.5% annually in a sample of 11 countries. The largest growth was seen in Ecuador (25%), Chile (12%), and Costa Rica and Mexico (9% each). In the smaller countries, these high growth rates came from an initially small number of

---

[4] Export SMEs are defined as firms exporting amounts of less than the respective country's per capita GDP, expressed in purchasing power parity (PPP), multiplied by 1,000 (Urmeneta, 2015).

exporters operating in that market. Few exporters in the region do business with China compared with other large markets: only 6.9% of exporters from 11 countries in the region in 2011 (see table II.2). However, China's share in the total value of exports is higher, as the average export value per company is greater than to the rest of the world.

Table II.2
Latin America (11 countries): export companies by destination, 2011
(Percentages of total export companies and number of exporters)

	Latin America	United States	European Union	China	Japan	Republic of Korea	Other	Number of exporters
Bolivia (Plurinational State of)	59.5	28.8	27.8	10.2	4.0	2.7	19.3	1 634
Brazil	62.9	33.9	37.4	13.8	8.9	5.4	27.0	19 194
Chile	69.3	29.2	30.4	11.1	7.4	7.5	24.9	7 634
Costa Rica	66.6	43.7	28.5	4.6	4.0	3.5	30.3	2 412
Ecuador	64.0	38.2	32.2	5.0	4.9	2.0	29.1	3 851
Guatemala	74.8	26.4	12.3	1.9	4.7	2.0	11.2	4 516
Mexico	29.4	73.2	15.6	4.7	3.2	2.2	16.5	35 694
Nicaragua	67.8	32.5	13.5	5.3	2.3	2.0	19.3	1 371
El Salvador	81.5	24.8	8.7	1.3	1.7	1.6	10.1	2 565
Peru	65.0 [a]	12.5	24.0 [a]	6.4	5.2	4.0	23.0 [a]	7 984
Uruguay	62.0	19.3	26.3	11.5	2.1	2.3	37.4	1 686
Total (11 countries)	63.9	33.0	23.3	6.9	4.4	3.2	22.6	88 541

Source: Economic Commission for Latin America and the Caribbean (ECLAC), on the basis of figures provided by the national customs offices of the respective countries.
Note: The sum of the percentages for each country exceeds 100%, as companies may export to more than one country at the same time.
[a] Estimates.

In the Chinese market, Latin American SME exporters are growing faster than the large exporters. Between 2007 and 2011, the number of SMEs in the region exporting to China grew faster than the number of large companies doing so. The value exported also grew faster for SMEs than for large exporters (see figure II.8).

FDI by China in Latin America and the Caribbean has been significant only since 2010, having reached a stock of US$ 7.336 billion in the two preceding decades (ECLAC, 2011).[5] That year marked a turning point, with an investment flow of close to US$ 14 billion, equivalent to 11% of total FDI in the region. In subsequent years, annual Chinese FDI has hovered between US$ 9 billion and US$ 10 billion (between 5% and 6% of the region's total inward FDI flows). Most of Chinese FDI flows to South America go to natural resource sectors (mining and hydrocarbons). In Mexico and, to a lesser extent, in Brazil, FDI also goes to manufacturing (automotive and electronic) and service industries, such as telecommunications, finance, energy distribution and retail commerce.

Conversely, FDI by Latin America in China is small-scale, accounting for only 0.25% of the region's total outward FDI between 2002 and 2011 and only 0.3% total FDI in China in 2012 and 2013.[6] This is due, in part, to the fact that the largest trans-Latin companies are concentrated in sectors (extractive and manufacturing activities based on natural resources) that are practically closed to FDI in China. Furthermore, most trans-Latin companies' foreign investment strategies have been based on reproducing the business model used in their home country, usually in neighbouring countries. The region's most significant investments in China have been made by the Brazilian manufacturing companies Marcopolo (bus bodywork) and Embraer (aeroplanes) and the Chilean company Molymet (molybdenum processing).

---

[5] Official data on Chinese FDI in the region do not capture its real extent, as Chinese companies often route much of their investments through third countries.

[6] See Estevadeordal, Mesquita Moreira and Kahn (2014) and FDI data from the National Bureau of Statistics of China [online] http://www.stats.gov.cn/tjsj/ndsj/2014/indexeh.htm [date of reference: 1 September 2015].

Figure II.8
**Latin America (10 countries): number of SMEs and large companies
exporting to China and export value, 2007 to 2011** [a]
(Index: 2007=100)

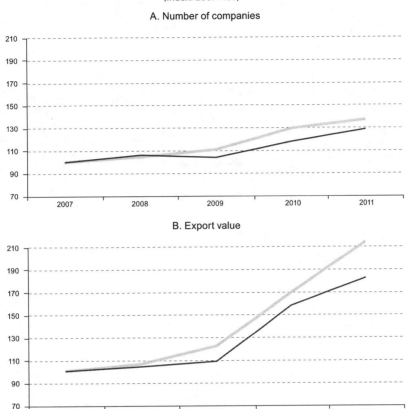

A. Number of companies

B. Export value

— Large companies ▬▬ SMEs

Source: Economic Commission for Latin America and the Caribbean (ECLAC), on the basis of figures provided by the national customs offices of Chile, Costa Rica, Ecuador, El Salvador, Guatemala, Mexico, Paraguay, Peru, Plurinational State of Bolivia and Uruguay.

[a] Export SMEs are defined as firms exporting amounts of less than the respective country's per capita GDP, expressed in purchasing power parity (PPP), multiplied by 1,000.

3. Bilateral production linkages are weak

With the exception of Mexico, Latin American countries participate little in global value chains and production integration is limited in the region (Durán and Zaclicever, 2013; ECLAC, 2014c), in contrast to China's strong integration in "Factory Asia".

A country's level of integration in global value chains can be measured through a participation index, which is expressed as a percentage of gross exports. The proportion of foreign value added contained in a country's gross exports measures its backward participation in value chains, while the proportion of domestic value added embedded in exports from other countries shows its forward participation (Bohn and others, 2015). Figure II.9 shows that the global value chain participation of six countries in Latin America was lower than that of Asia in 2011 (41% and 52%, respectively). This is due to the fact that Latin American exports make less intensive use of imported inputs, in other words, they have fewer backward linkages (20% as against 30% in Asia).[7] If Mexico is excluded, the region's global participation index falls to 38%, owing to less backward participation (13% in 2011) that is only partly offset by increased forward participation (25% in 2011).

---

[7] Analysis based on multi-country Trade in Value Added (TiVA) input-output tables from the Organization for Economic Cooperation and Development (OECD) and World Trade Organization (WTO). The 2015 version includes six Latin American countries: Argentina, Brazil, Chile, Colombia, Costa Rica and Mexico (see [online] http://www.oecd.org/sti/ind/measuringtradeinvalue-addedanoecd-wtojointinitiative.htm). The Asian region includes Brunei Darussalam, Cambodia, China, Hong Kong (SAR of China), India, Indonesia, Japan, Malaysia, the Philippines, Republic of Korea, Singapore, Taiwan Province of China, Thailand and Viet Nam.

Figure II.9
**Selected regions and countries: forward and backward participation
in global value chains, 2000 and 2011**
(Percentages of gross exports)

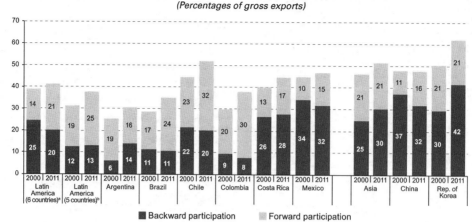

■ Backward participation   ▦ Forward participation

Source: Economic Commission for Latin America and the Caribbean (ECLAC), on the basis of Organization for Economic Cooperation and Development (OECD)/
World Trade Organization (WTO), Trade in Value-Added Database (TiVA) [online] http://www.oecd.org/sti/ind/measuringtradeinvalue-addedanoecd-
wtojointinitiative.htm.
a Argentina, Brazil, Chile, Colombia, Costa Rica and Mexico.
b Argentina, Brazil, Chile, Colombia and Costa Rica.

Of the six Latin American countries examined, Mexico uses the most imported inputs in its exports, followed by Costa Rica (with backward value chain participation indices of 32% and 28%, respectively). Chile and Colombia have the highest level of forward participation in the region (32% and 30%, respectively, in 2011), reflecting greater integration as suppliers of inputs. Mexico's and Costa Rica's degree of linkage is comparable to China's, although much less than the Republic of Korea's (which has strong backward participation in global value chains). Colombia, Brazil and Argentina have lower levels of backward linkages than China, while their forward linkages are generally higher.

The global value chain participation profile reflects each country's export specialization. Countries that specialize in exporting commodities and commodity-based manufactures, such as Argentina, Brazil, Chile and Colombia, have lower levels of backward participation in global value chains, since this type of unprocessed good uses fewer imported inputs. Conversely, they tend to have strong forward linkages, as they are used in the early stages of value chains. On the other hand, countries such as China, Costa Rica, Mexico and the Republic of Korea that export mostly manufactures not based on natural resources tend to use more imported inputs in their exports (reflected in a lower proportion of domestic value added) and have weaker forward linkages.

In 2000, every country shown in figure II.9 (except China) increased its global value chain participation index, as a result of the increasing international fragmentation of production. For the most part, Latin American countries' forward participation has increased and their backward linkages have decreased, possibly resulting from growth in exports of commodities and related products. The exceptions are Argentina, which sharply increased its backward linkages (although still at low levels) and reduced its forward linkages, and Costa Rica, which showed a rise in both types of participation. China maintained its global value chain participation index but the composition of its linkages shifted: less foreign value added in its exports, offset by an increase in the proportion of value added exported by China that becomes embedded in the exports of third countries.

Analysis of the geographical origin of value added in exports reveals significant differences between Latin American countries and China (see figure II.10). The United States and the European Union are major providers of inputs for the exports of the six Latin American countries examined. The United States is the largest supplier for Mexico and Costa Rica (with around 40% of both countries' total foreign value added in 2011), and other countries within the region supply only a small proportion (especially in Mexico). Exports by Argentina and Chile, however, show a larger proportion of value added originating in other countries within the region (around 30% of both countries' totals in 2011).

Figure II.10
Selected regions and countries: gross export structure
by origin of value added, 2011
(Percentages of total)

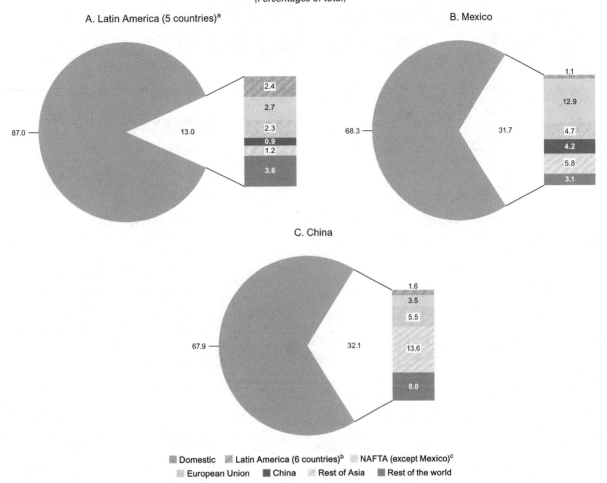

Source: Economic Commission for Latin America and the Caribbean (ECLAC), on the basis of Organization for Economic Cooperation and Development (OECD)/World Trade Organization (WTO), Trade in Value-Added Database (TiVA) [online] http://www.oecd.org/sti/ind/measuringtradeinvalue-addedanoecd-wtojointinitiative.htm.
a Argentina, Brazil, Chile, Colombia and Costa Rica.
b Argentina, Brazil, Chile, Colombia, Costa Rica and Mexico.
c North American Free Trade Agreement.

China's forward linkages with Latin American countries are growing. Its share of foreign value added in Mexican exports rose from 1.3% in 2000 to 13.2% in 2011, to the detriment of the United States, whose share fell from 60% to 37%. China's share in the exports of the rest of the Latin American countries is also increasing. At the same time, the Latin American countries have considerably increased their own share of the foreign value added exported by China, although the figure remains low (around 5% in 2011). China's backward linkages are mainly within Asia, which accounts for 42% of the total foreign value added in China's exports.

Analysis of the composition of forward linkages also shows growing links between Latin American countries and China (see figure II.11). In Mexico, these linkages are mostly with its partners in the North American Free Trade Agreement (NAFTA), particularly with the United States, but Asia accounts for a significant proportion (China in particular, rising from 2% in 2000 to almost 8% in 2011). The rest of the Latin American countries export domestic value added chiefly to Asia (around 40% in 2011), particularly China, which increased its share from 6% to 19% between 2000 and 2011.

Figure II.11
Selected regions and countries: structure of forward global value chain participation, by exporting region, 2011
(Percentages of the total)

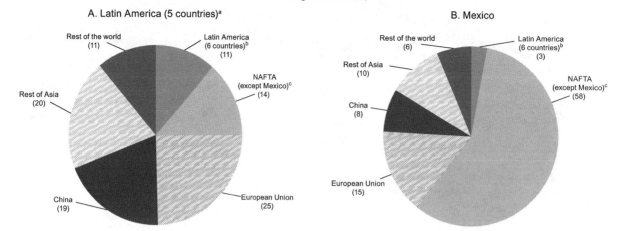

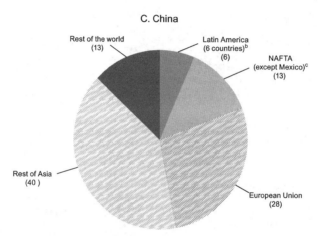

Source: Economic Commission for Latin America and the Caribbean (ECLAC), on the basis of Organization for Economic Cooperation and Development (OECD)/World Trade Organization (WTO), Trade in Value-Added Database (TiVA) [online] http://www.oecd.org/sti/ind/measuringtradeinvalue-addedanoecd-wtojointinitiative.htm.
[a] Argentina, Brazil, Chile, Colombia and Costa Rica.
[b] Argentina, Brazil, Chile, Colombia, Costa Rica and Mexico.
[c] North American Free Trade Agreement.

Latin American countries' share in China's forward linkages has also risen significantly, albeit from very low levels (from 3% in 2000 to 6% in 2011). Like its backward linkages, China's forward linkages are concentrated in the Asian region.

In sum, value chain linkages between Latin American countries and China have increased, both forward and backward. However, the sectoral composition of these linkages reflects the trade structure between the two partners, with the forward linkages of Latin American countries becoming increasingly concentrated in commodities and natural-resource-based manufactures (see table II.3). Until recently, Costa Rica was the exception, since a large proportion of its domestic value added embedded in China's exports came from the electronics sector. This is no longer the case, however, since the closure of the INTEL microprocessor assembly plant in Costa Rica in 2015.

With regard to services, retail commerce stands out as being among the three sectors having most forward linkages with China in 2011. The other two were transport and storage services (accounting for between 4% of the domestic value added embedded in Chinese exports for Colombia and 9% for Costa Rica) and research and development (R&D) and other business services (with 3% of the local value added in China's exports for Colombia and 8% for Brazil).

Table II.3
Latin America (6 countries): main sectors of origin of domestic
value added embedded in Chinese exports, 2000 and 2011

Country [a]	Main sector	Second sector	Third sector
Argentina (6%)	Agriculture, forestry and fishing (33% in 2011 and 17% in 2000)	Wholesale and retail trade (15% in 2011 and 24% in 2000)	Mining (14% in 2011 and 13% in 2000)
Brazil (46%)	Mining (27% in 2011 and 10% in 2000)	Wholesale and retail trade (18% in 2011 and 16% in 2000)	Agriculture, forestry and fishing (10% in 2011 and 11% in 2000)
Chile (28%)	Basic metals (53% in 2011 and 38% in 2000)	Mining (14% in 2011 and 8% in 2000)	Wholesale and retail trade (7% in 2011 and 10% 2000)
Colombia (5%)	Mining (61% in 2011 and 33% in 2000)	Wholesale and retail trade (10% in 2011 and 15% in 2000)	Basic metals (10% in 2011 and 6% in 2000)
Costa Rica (2%)	Computing and electronic and optical equipment (29% in 2011 and 31% in 2000)	Wholesale and retail trade (21% in 2011 and 16% in 2000)	Transport and storage (9% in 2011 and 16% in 2000)
Mexico (13%)	Mining (35% in 2011 and 12% in 2000)	Wholesale and retail trade (18% in 2011 and 18% in 2000)	Basic metals (9% in 2011 and 4% in 2000)

Source: Economic Commission for Latin America and the Caribbean (ECLAC), on the basis of Organization for Economic Cooperation and Development (OECD)/World Trade Organization (WTO), Trade in Value-Added Database (TiVA) [online] http://www.oecd.org/sti/ind/measuringtradeinvalue-addedanoecd-wtojointinitiative.htm.
[a] The percentage shown in brackets beside the name of each country in the left-hand column corresponds to its share in the combined value added of the six countries embedded in Chinese exports in 2011.

C. Diversifying trade and investment is an imperative

1. Embed more technology and knowledge into regional exports

The rise and diversification of regional exports to China requires policies aimed at developing new sectors, products and services. Although the depreciation of several Latin American currencies in recent months could encourage the diversification of exports to China, the concentrated regional production and export structure limits that possibility. Market signals are unlikely to be enough to reduce export concentration very much. Rather, what are needed are policies for building production capacities. China's own experience testifies to this, as a country that has built up dynamic comparative advantages on the basis of a long-term vision and has accordingly been able to gradually climb the ladder of technological complexity. Thanks to high expenditure on R&D (2% of GDP in 2012), China came to account for 32% of worldwide patent applications in 2013, displacing the United States as the global leader. This has reduced its dependence on low-cost labour and positioned it among the new technological paradigms, through active pursuit of smart manufacturing.

Analysis of the Chinese experience could be useful for creating and implementing long-term policies for building dynamic comparative advantages in Latin America and the Caribbean. An example is skills-building through improvements in the quality of education at all levels and its links to the labour market. The shortages in the region's labour force in areas such as science, technology, engineering and mathematics are well known. Surveys carried out by the World Bank indicate that 36% of companies in the region consider the lack of skilled labour a major growth constraint. In China, only 2% of companies shared this opinion (CAF/ECLAC/OECD, 2015).

Together with efforts to create new exportable goods and services, in the short term, countries in the region should try to capitalize on the great potential that some of its existing products have in the Chinese market. This potential is evident in the goods and services for which demand has surged in the past decade, as well as those whose consumption could increase rapidly as a result of economic reforms and other changes under way in China.

Agriculture and agro-industry is a promising sector, as China needs to feed 19% of the world's population with only 7% of its farmland and 6% of its water resources. Between 2000 and 2013, China's food imports grew by 21% per year on average (see figure II.12). In 2004, China became a net food importer and since then its agriculture trade deficit has widened. If this trend continues, China's food imports will more than double by 2020 along with the steady expansion of the middle classes and reforms geared towards boosting consumption.

Figure II.12
China: food imports, 2000-2013
(Billions of dollars)

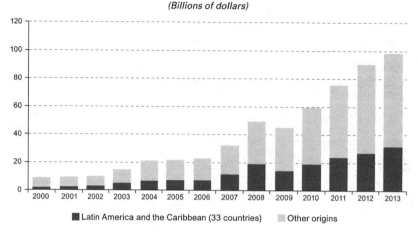

■ Latin America and the Caribbean (33 countries)   ▢ Other origins

Source: Economic Commission for Latin America and the Caribbean (ECLAC), on the basis of information from the United Nations Commodity Trade Statistics Database (COMTRADE).
Note: Based on revision 2 of the Standard International Trade Classification (SITC), products from sectors 0 (food products), 1 (tobacco and beverages), 22 (seeds and fruit) and 4 (animal and vegetable oils).

Latin American agricultural and food exports to China have grown rapidly, but the very high concentration of products and countries of origin diminishes the benefits for the region as a whole. China's share of Latin America's agricultural and food exports rose from 1.2% in 1990 to 12.9% in 2014. At the same time, the region's share in Chinese imports of agricultural products shot up from 16% in 2000 to 27% in 2014. However, agricultural exports to China are even more concentrated than total exports, as a single product (soybeans) accounted for 78% of the total export value in 2014. All processed products, except soybean oil, form a tiny proportion of the basket of exports to China. Just one country, Brazil, was the source of 75% of the region's agricultural exports to China in 2014 and, if Argentina, Chile and Uruguay are included alongside Brazil, these four countries account for 98% of the region's agricultural exports.

Latin American and Caribbean countries have the potential to become strategic partners for China in the agrifood market. They have not only vast natural and water resources, but also international companies that are competitive in the different segments of the agro-industrial chain. This places the region in good stead to become a major supplier of nutritious, safe and high-quality foods, and diversify from reliance on exports of agricultural commodities. Opportunities abound, not only to increase and diversify exports to China, but also for trans-Latin companies to invest there, tapping their food industry expertise to supply local markets and use China as an export platform for the rest of Asia.

The China-Latin America and the Caribbean Agricultural Ministers' Forum, established in Beijing in June 2013, is a suitable sphere for exploring ways to expand trade between the two parties. Its members agreed to work together to facilitate agricultural trade by eliminating tariff and non-tariff barriers and expediting procedures for approving sanitary and phytosanitary permits. The Forum could also be an ideal platform to promote knowledge and technology exchange and partnerships between agrifood enterprises in China and the region (ECLAC, 2015a).

In the services sector, tourism is an area with great potential. According to the World Tourism Organization (UNWTO), Chinese tourists will number 100 million in 2015. Despite the fact that Chinese tourists spent more abroad than any other nationality in 2012, Latin America and the Caribbean only received 251,000 visitors from China in 2013 (see figure II.13), owing partly to strict entry visa requirements. Cooperation between the governments of the region and China in this area could, therefore, help to attract a greater number of visitors.[8] Other factors behind the small number of Chinese visitors to the region could be the lack of air links and the limited supply of package holidays and other services suitable for Chinese demand.

---

[8]   Some Latin American countries have recently removed visa requirements for Chinese visitors or allow free entry to Chinese holders of visas for the United States or for a member country of the Schengen Convention.

Figure II.13
Latin America and China: bilateral visits, 2013

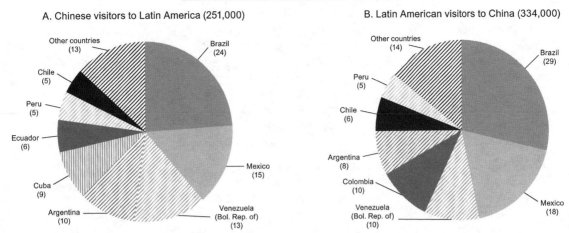

A. Chinese visitors to Latin America (251,000)

B. Latin American visitors to China (334,000)

Source: Economic Commission for Latin America and the Caribbean (ECLAC), on the basis of figures provided by the World Tourism Organization (UNWTO).

The creation of regional trade and investment facilitation centres in Beijing and other Chinese cities could contribute to the diversification of exports and promote reciprocal FDI. These centres could carry out different functions to benefit the entire region, such as improving knowledge about the impact of economic reforms and new consumption trends, promoting partnerships between companies in the region and their Chinese counterparts, providing institutional support to facilitate dialogue with Chinese authorities, removing barriers to trade and investment and promoting business opportunities in Latin America (ECLAC, 2015b).

The governments of Latin America and China could also sign and expand plurinational agreements on trade, tax and legal matters to streamline trade and business with China, which has already signed free trade agreements (FTAs) with Chile (2006), Peru (2010) and Costa Rica (2011) and double taxation treaties with nine countries in Latin America and the Caribbean.[9]

2. Expand and improve the quality of reciprocal foreign direct investment flows

The reforms already under way in China could boost FDI flows into Latin America and the Caribbean. Slower investment growth, increasing labour costs and the search for investment opportunities for surplus savings should encourage China to spend more abroad, in line with the government's indications. Latin America, in turn, offers interesting investment opportunities: large consumer markets, proximity and preferential access of some of the region's economies to the United States market and an abundance of natural resources.

It is important for the region not only to attract greater FDI inflows from China, but also to promote sectoral diversification and linkages with local companies. Given that almost 90% of Chinese FDI in the region between 2010 and 2013 went to natural resources, particularly mining and hydrocarbons, boosting flows of capital towards sectors such as manufactures and services would diversify the region's production structure, especially if that FDI were linked with local supply networks. This poses a twofold policy challenge for the region. On one hand, national investment promotion agencies must actively disseminate existing investment opportunities in each country, as well as share information about respective regulatory frameworks. On the other hand, policies must be reinforced to achieve a critical mass of local companies capable of supplying goods and services to new Chinese companies (and those of other nationalities) investing in the region. In this regard, it is important to strengthen supplier development programmes, which can be an effective tool for promoting indirect internationalization, particularly for SMEs.

---

9 These nine countries are: Brazil (1991), Jamaica (1996), Barbados (2000), Cuba (2001), Bolivarian Republic of Venezuela (2001), Trinidad and Tobago (2003), Mexico (2005), Ecuador (2013) and Chile (2015). For more information see [online] http://www.chinatax.gov.cn/2013/n2925/n2955/index.html [date of reference: 21 August 2015].

Chinese investment could also help overcome the region's infrastructure deficits. The limited involvement of Latin America and the Caribbean in global value chains is partly due to high non-tariff trade costs. The tariff equivalent of these costs in 2013 was 125% in Latin America, compared with 98% in East Asia. Latin America also has one of the highest intraregional trade costs, with a tariff equivalent of 113%, compared with 84% in East Asia (OECD/WTO, 2015), owing mainly to underdeveloped transport and logistical infrastructure. China's government and businesses have recently shown interest in exploring the feasibility of large-scale infrastructure projects in the region —for example, a railway linking the Atlantic and Pacific costs of South America. If the projects undertaken were consistent with the priorities set out by the countries of the region in forums such as the South American Infrastructure and Planning Council (COSIPLAN) of the Union of South American Nations (UNASUR) and the Meso-America Project, Chinese capital could make a significant contribution to closing the region's infrastructure gap. The funding for these projects would be particularly useful given the reduced fiscal space now available to the countries of the region.

Making good use of the business opportunities arising in China in the coming years will require increased FDI by Latin America in China, to bring Latin American companies closer to their final consumers and respond faster and more efficiently to their demands. Therefore, as well as promoting diversification of goods exports to China, the governments of the region should support the direct presence of Latin American companies in that market. Lessons can be drawn from the pioneering experiences of trans-Latin companies already operating in China. It will also be important to keep track of the opportunities arising from initiatives such as the free trade areas created in some cities (Shanghai, and similar projects in Guangdong, Tianjin and Fujian).

Because they are highly concentrated in commodities, Latin America's exports to China generate a greater environmental impact than the region's exports to the rest of the world. The region's sales to China consist mainly of minerals and metals, oil and agricultural products such as soybeans. These sectors are environmentally sensitive because of their high water intensity and greenhouse gas emissions. Exports to China thus consume more than twice as much water and emit more greenhouse gases for every dollar exported than the region's average exports to the rest of the world (see figure II.14).

Figure II.14
Latin America: environmental impact of exports,
worldwide and to China, 2004

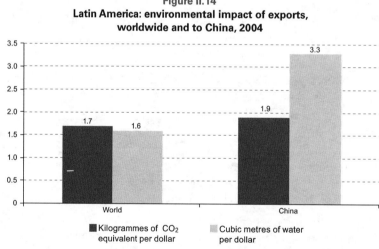

Source: Economic Commission for Latin America and the Caribbean (ECLAC), on the basis of Rebecca Ray and others, *China in Latin America: Lessons for South-South Cooperation and Sustainable Development*, Boston University, Centro de Investigación para la Transformación, Tufts University and Universidad del Pacífico, 2015.

The concentration of Chinese FDI in the mining and hydrocarbon sectors has resulted in socio-environmental conflicts in some countries. These episodes are largely due to several weaknesses in the governance of natural resources in the host countries: weak regulatory frameworks with insufficient oversight, conflicts between different levels of government and inadequate or non-existent consultation mechanisms with the local communities affected. Chinese companies, whose presence in the region is relatively recent compared with other countries, also lack familiarity with the policy framework and other circumstances (for example, cultural issues) in the countries where they invest.

The challenge of making Chinese investment more socially and environmentally sustainable requires commitment from all the parties involved. Governments in the region must build up their regulatory frameworks for investment (local and foreign alike) in extractive activities and other sectors with a strong environmental impact, such as infrastructure and industry. They also need better coordination between the different levels of government involved in projects and better mechanisms for consultation with local communities. Chinese firms, for their part, should redouble their efforts not only to comply with regulatory frameworks in the countries where they invest, but also to adapt to local customs and practice. They should also increase efforts to hire and train workers from the areas where they invest, and to generate linkages with local suppliers. Lastly, the Government of China could strengthen mechanisms to ensure compliance with the various guidelines developed over the past 20 years for Chinese firms investing abroad (ECLAC, 2015a).[10]

3. Progress toward a more integrated regional market and a common strategy for China

The region will become a more attractive partner for China if it speeds up and deepens its economic integration process. Despite the advances made in the reduction of tariff barriers to intraregional trade, there is still significant heterogeneity among the national and subnational regulatory frameworks in areas such as treatment of foreign investment and services, public procurement, technical regulations, intellectual property, competition policy and border procedures. This fragmentation of the regional market makes it difficult to create production linkages between Latin American companies and also gain a larger share of global value chains. As a result, a gradual harmonization of the different regulatory regimes that affect the working of the region's production networks must be promoted. This would not only incentivize intraregional trade and investment flows, but would also help to attract FDI inflows aimed at taking advantage of the enlarged regional market.

The current rebalancing process of the Chinese growth model and the end of the commodities boom mark a turning point in the economic relationship between Latin America and China. The new stage provides opportunities and challenges for both parties. Although regional exports to China are not expected to grow as fast in the coming years as they did throughout most of the last decade, opportunities will arise to shift sales toward goods and services with greater value added. Furthermore, if the region attracts more FDI flows from China to new sectors, the economic and trade relationship between the two regions could be drastically redefined. A stronger presence from Chinese companies in industries such as automotive, agroindustrial or electronics, linked with local suppliers, could strengthen regional production integration and increase the region's share in global value chains.

The Government of China recognizes the strategic importance of its links with Latin America and the Caribbean and has accordingly made it a priority to find institutional mechanisms for dialogue with the region. In January 2015, China agreed upon a cooperation plan for 2015-2019 with the members of the Community of Latin American and Caribbean States (CELAC), which is structured around a "1+3+6" framework that aims to achieve inclusive growth and sustainable development through three engines (trade, investment and cooperation) and six areas of work (energy and resources, infrastructure, agriculture, manufacturing, technological innovation and information technologies). The 2015-2019 CELAC-China cooperation plan provides an appropriate institutional framework to progress in all areas of mutual interest. Both parties must now agree upon mutually beneficial actions in order to given this cooperation concrete form.

The challenge for Latin America and the Caribbean is to produce a regional response to the initiatives proposed by China. Although this effort is complicated by the heterogeneity of the region, there are shared areas of interest in which common positions can realistically be adopted. Such is the case with initiatives that seek to diversify exports and Chinese FDI in the region, promote joint research, attract more tourists and close the regional infrastructure gap.

---

[10] In particular, "Guidelines for environmental protection in foreign investment and cooperation", which was published jointly by the Ministries of Trade and Environmental Protection of China in February 2013.

Bibliography

Bohn, T. and others (2015), "Integration into global value chains: A guide to data sources and indicators", *OECD Trade Policy Papers*, forthcoming.

CAF/ECLAC/OECD (Latin American Development Bank/Economic Commission for Latin America and the Caribbean/ Organization for Economic Co-operation and Development) (2015), *Latin American Economic Outlook 2016*, Paris (forthcoming).

Durán Lima, J. and D. Zaclicever (2013), "América Latina y el Caribe en las cadenas internacionales de valor", *Comercio Internacional series*, No. 124 (C/L.3767), Santiago, Economic Commission for Latin America and the Caribbean (ECLAC).

ECLAC (Economic Commission for Latin America and the Caribbean) (2015a), *Latin America and the Caribbean and China: Towards a new era in economic cooperation* (LC/L.4010), Santiago, May.

___ (2015b), *Economic Relations between Latin America and the Caribbean and the Republic of Korea: Advances and opportunities* (LC/L.3994), Santiago.

___ (2014a), *Latin America and the Caribbean in the World Economy 2014: Regional integration and value chains in a challenging external environment* (LC/G.2625-P), Santiago.

___ (2014b), *International trade and inclusive development: Building synergies* (LC/G.2562), Santiago.

___ (2014c), *Regional integration: Towards a strategy for inclusive value chain* (LC/G.2594(SES.35/11)), Santiago.

___ (2014d), *Cadenas globales de valor y diversificación de exportaciones: el caso de Costa Rica* (LC/L.3804), Santiago, abril.

___ (2014e), *Urbanización y políticas de vivienda en China y América Latina y el Caribe. Perspectivas y estudios de caso* (LC/L.3939), Santiago, Chinese Academy of Social Sciences (CASS)/Development Bank of Latin America (CAF).

___ (2013), *Latin America and the Caribbean in the World Economy 2013: A sluggish postcrisis, mega trade negotiations and value chains: scope for regional action* (LC/G.2578-P), Santiago.

___ (2011), *Foreign Direct Investment in Latin America and the Caribbean, 2010* (LC/G.2494-P), Santiago.

Estevadeordal, Antoni, Mauricio Mesquita Moreira and Theodore Kahn (2014), *LAC Investment in China: A new chapter in Latin America and the Caribbean-China relations*, Washington, D.C., Inter-American Development Bank (IDB).

OECD/WTO (Organization for Economic Cooperation and Development/World Trade Organization) (2015), *Aid for Trade at a Glance 2015: Reducing trade costs for inclusive, sustainable growth*, Paris, OECD Publishing.

Ray, Rebecca and others (2015), *China in Latin America: Lessons for South-South Cooperation and Sustainable Development*, Boston University, Centro de Investigación para la Transformación, Tufts University and Universidad del Pacífico.

Rosales, Osvaldo, Keiji Inoue y Nanno Mulder (editors) (2015), *Rising Concentration in Asia-Latin American Value Chains: Can small firms turn the tide?*, ECLAC Books, No. 135 (LC/G.2642-P), Santiago, Economic Commission for Latin America and the Caribbean (ECLAC).

The Wall Street Journal (2012), "Chasing China's shoppers", 14 June.

United States Grains Council (2011), *Food 2040. The future of food and agriculture in East Asia* [online] http://www.grains.org/ sites/default/files/pdfs/US-Grains-Council-Food-2040-Report-FINAL.pdf.

Urmeneta, Roberto (2015), "Dinámica de las empresas exportadoras en América Latina: relevancia de las pymes", *Project Dcuments*, Santiago, Economic Commission for Latin America and the Caribbean (ECLAC), forthcoming.

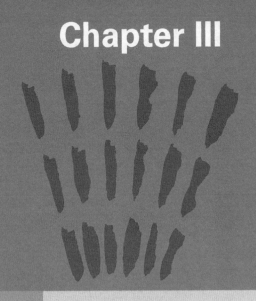

Chapter III

Latin America and the Caribbean needs to move forward with the trade facilitation agenda

A. Trade facilitation reduces costs and saves time

Trade facilitation has been increasingly to the fore on policy agendas because it offers a way of better integrating countries into world trade. This trend has been reinforced by the development of international production networks (also known as regional or global value chains) and the conclusion of the World Trade Organization (WTO) Trade Facilitation Agreement (TFA) in December 2013. The present chapter examines the implementation of this agenda in Latin America and the Caribbean and the resulting policy issues.

According to WTO, trade facilitation is the "simplification and harmonization of international trade procedures", i.e. "the activities, practices and formalities involved in collecting, presenting, communicating and processing data and other information required for the movement of goods in international trade".[1] The Asia-Pacific Economic Cooperation (APEC) forum and the United Nations Conference on Trade and Development (UNCTAD) use broader definitions that include elements such as the availability of transport and telecommunications infrastructure and logistical services.

Although physical infrastructure strongly affects the flow of international trade, this chapter focuses on customs and other procedures that economic agents must follow to carry out export and import operations. This approach mirrors that of the new TFA, whose provisions will gradually become enforceable for all countries of the region when it enters into force (see annex III.A1). The trade facilitation agenda includes five groups of measures: transparency, formalities, institutional arrangements and cooperation, paperless trade, and transit facilitation (see annex III.A2).

A first estimate for the scale of the costs that customs and other formalities impose on international trade can be obtained from the results of the World Bank study *Doing Business 2015: Going Beyond Efficiency*. It is clear from this study that the costs of foreign trade operations and the time and number of documents required vary greatly from country to country (see table III.1). In general, the countries where importing and exporting are most expensive and time-consuming also require the most documents.

Table III.1
Lowest and highest values for the number of documents, time and cost involved in exporting and importing a 20-foot container by sea, 2014

Variable	Importing		Exporting	
	Lowest	Highest	Lowest	Highest
Documents *(number)*	2	17	2	11
Time *(days)*	4	130	6	86
Cost *(dollars)*	415	10 650	410	9 050

Source: Economic Commission for Latin America and the Caribbean (ECLAC), on the basis of World Bank, *Doing Business 2015: Going Beyond Efficiency*, Washington, D.C., 2015 [online] www.doingbusiness.org/reports/global-reports/doing-business-2015.

Although the results are better for Latin America and the Caribbean than for other developing regions such as sub-Saharan Africa and South and Central Asia, the region is struggling to reduce non-tariff costs and the time taken by foreign trade operations. Its performance in this area is poorer than that of the developed countries and those of East and South-East Asia (see figure III.1). This is due to a shortage of economic infrastructure, including transport infrastructure (Lardé and Sánchez, 2014; IDB, 2013), and inefficient administrative procedures. Costs are particularly high in the Caribbean. In all three subregions, it is cheaper to trade with the United States than within each subregion (see table III.2).

---

[1] See [online] http://gtad.wto.org/trta_subcategory.aspx?cat=33121.

Figure III.1

Selected regions and groupings: cost of exporting and importing a container, 2014 [a]

(Dollars)

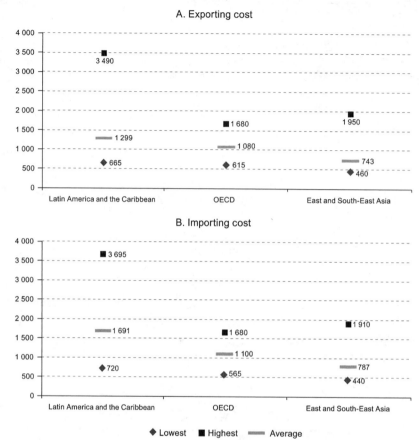

A. Exporting cost

B. Importing cost

◆ Lowest ■ Highest ▬ Average

Source: Economic Commission for Latin America and the Caribbean (ECLAC), on the basis of World Bank, *Doing Business 2015: Going Beyond Efficiency*, Washington, D.C., 2015 [online] www.doingbusiness.org/reports/global-reports/doing-business-2015.

[a] East and South-East Asia includes China, Taiwan Province of China, Hong Kong Special Administrative Region of China and the 10 member States of the Association of Southeast Asian Nations (ASEAN). Japan and the Republic of Korea are included in the Organization for Economic Cooperation and Development (OECD) group.

Table III.2

Selected country groupings: average cost of trade within and outside the grouping (excluding tariffs), 2008-2013

(Percentage tariff equivalents)

Grouping	Caribbean (2 countries) [a]	Central America and Mexico (3 countries) [b]	South America (4 countries) [c]	ASEAN (4 countries) [d]	European Union (3 countries) [e]
The Caribbean [a]	154				
Central America and Mexico [b]	160	88			
South America [c]	218	124	91		
Association of Southeast Asian Nations (ASEAN) [d]	301	200	155	76	
European Union [e]	178	152	115	108	43
United States	89	66	84	85	67

Source: Economic Commission for Latin America and the Caribbean (ECLAC), on the basis of information from the World Bank/Economic and Social Commission for Asia and the Pacific (ESCAP) International Trade Costs database [online] http://databank.worldbank.org/data/reports.aspx?source=escap-world-bank:-international-trade-costs.

[a] Dominican Republic and Jamaica.

[b] Costa Rica, Guatemala and Mexico.

[c] Argentina, Brazil, Chile and Colombia.

[d] Indonesia, Malaysia, the Philippines and Thailand.

[e] France, Germany and United Kingdom.

The impact of implementing specific trade facilitation measures for trade flows and their associated costs is quantified in OECD (2015). Using information on the extent of implementation of 11 indicators in 152 countries, its estimates indicate that full implementation of the TFA, including not only mandatory provisions but also voluntary ones, could reduce trade-related costs by between 12% and 17%, depending on countries' income level. If implementation were limited to the mandatory provisions, cost savings would be smaller at all income levels (see table III.3). The difference between the two scenarios is particularly pronounced for low and lower-middle income countries, since many higher income countries are already implementing several of the voluntary provisions. With regard to the type of measures, costs would be reduced the most by improving trade-related formalities, and in particular by harmonizing and simplifying documents and automating customs procedures.

Table III.3
Estimated reduction in trade costs from implementing the Trade Facilitation Agreement
(Percentages)

	Low income countries	Lower-middle income countries	Upper-middle income countries	OECD countries
Full implementation	16.5	17.4	14.6	11.8
Implementation of mandatory provisions only	12.6	13.7	12.8	10.4

Source: Organization for Economic Cooperation and Development (OECD), "Implementation of the WTO Trade Facilitation Agreement: The potential impact on trade costs", Paris, June 2015 [online] http://www.oecd.org/tad/tradedev/WTO-TF-Implementation-Policy-Brief_EN_2015_06.pdf.

A study analysing the potential impact of trade facilitation on 107 developing countries indicated that the measures which would have the greatest effect on trade flows in Latin America and the Caribbean were simplifying formalities, making relevant information available, issuing advance rulings and applying transparent and proportional fees and charges. The measures that would reduce costs the most in the region were expediting border procedures, issuing advance rulings and harmonizing and simplifying the documents required (Moisé and Sorescu, 2013).

B. The region is moving forward, but at different speeds

Given the significant effects of trade facilitation on trade flows and the cost of export, import and transit operations, progress in Latin America and the Caribbean needs to be assessed on different analytical levels, namely for the region as a whole, its subregions and its individual countries, and for each category of measures. This section contains a brief overview of the results of a survey on the implementation of trade facilitation measures carried out by ECLAC among government bodies, particularly customs authorities and ministries of trade and industry, in 19 countries of the region between November 2014 and July 2015.[2]

Each country was asked whether each trade facilitation measure had been fully implemented, partially implemented, was in the pilot stage or had not been implemented. Following independent verification, each response was given a predefined value to enable comparisons among the countries of the region and with the other regions in the Global Survey. For each measure, the answer "fully implemented" received three points, "partially implemented" two points, "pilot stage" one point and "not implemented" zero points. The total score for each country is the sum of the scores for each of the 30 questions.

---

[2] This survey is part of the Global Survey on Trade Facilitation and Paperless Trade Implementation 2015, a project of the five United Nations regional commissions. The results of the survey for Latin America and the Caribbean are presented in full in García and Herreros (2015).

1. The Caribbean lags behind South America and Central America and Mexico

The region has made considerable progress in implementing trade facilitation measures, with an average of 68% of the maximum possible score (see figure III.2). This regional average is close to the results of Asian countries that took part in the Global Survey, such as India, Malaysia and the Philippines (Duval, Wang and Tsoulou Malakoudi, 2015).

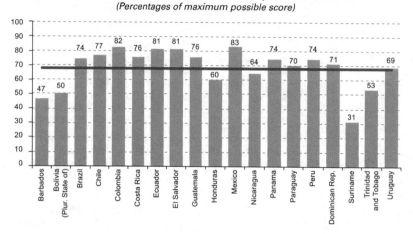

Figure III.2

Latin America and the Caribbean (19 countries): total scores in the Global Survey on Trade Facilitation and Paperless Trade Implementation 2015 [a]

(Percentages of maximum possible score)

Source: Economic Commission for Latin America and the Caribbean (ECLAC), on the basis of information from the Global Survey on Trade Facilitation and Paperless Trade Implementation 2015.

[a] The horizontal line represents the average for the 19 countries (68%).

The scores of 13 of the 19 countries replying to the questionnaire were above the regional average. The same was true of 7 of the 8 South American countries that participated and 5 of the 7 countries in the Central America and Mexico subregion. In the Caribbean, only the Dominican Republic scored above the regional average, while the scores of the other three countries that participated were well below the average. By subregion, Central America and Mexico had the highest average implementation rate (74%), followed by South America (72%)[3] and the Caribbean (51%).

At the country level, Mexico and Colombia had the highest scores, while Suriname and Barbados had the lowest. Implementation rates in Mexico, Colombia, Ecuador and El Salvador were comparable to those of Australia, China, Japan, New Zealand, the Republic of Korea and Singapore, according to the Global Survey.

In general, there is a positive relationship between a country's score and its per capita gross domestic product (GDP), but there are exceptions. For example, Suriname had the lowest implementation rate of any of the 19 countries taking part in the survey even though it has a higher per capita GDP (measured in terms of purchasing power parity) than 13 of them. Similarly, Trinidad and Tobago scored lower than the regional mean despite being the country with the highest per capita GDP of the 19 questionnaire respondents. In contrast, Paraguay, Guatemala and particularly El Salvador scored above the regional average, despite having per capita incomes well below the mean for the participating countries (see figure III.3). This indicates that a country's performance is influenced by variables other than per capita GDP including, most notably, the size of its economy, its geography (for example, island nation or landlocked), its institutional capacities and whether it is a party to trade agreements or economic integration mechanisms involving trade facilitation commitments.

The high implementation rates in Central American countries are largely the result of a common legal framework, the Uniform Central American Customs Code (CAUCA), which has permitted harmonization and simplification of export and import procedures and cross-border electronic sharing of documentation. Another factor contributing to

---

[3] The results for South America do not include Argentina or the Bolivarian Republic of Venezuela.

this good performance has been the signing by Central American countries of a free trade agreement with the United States (the Dominican Republic-Central America-United States Free Trade Agreement (CAFTA-DR)) and an association agreement with the European Union (to which Panama is also a signatory). Both instruments contain chapters on trade facilitation that are broad in scope. A significant role is also played by international cooperation received by the subregion in the area of trade facilitation, particularly under the European Union Regional Project for Support of Central American Economic Integration and Implementation of the Association Agreement (PRAIAA).

Figure III.3
Latin America and the Caribbean (19 countries): per capita gross domestic product (GDP) in 2013 and total score in the Global Survey on Trade Facilitation and Paperless Trade Implementation 2015 [a]
(Dollars and percentages of maximum possible score)

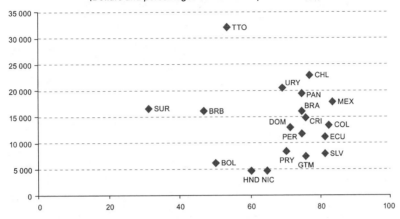

Source: Economic Commission for Latin America and the Caribbean (ECLAC), on the basis of information from the Global Survey on Trade Facilitation and Paperless Trade Implementation 2015 and International Monetary Fund (IMF), World Economic Outlook (WEO) database, April 2015 [online] https://www.imf.org/external/pubs/ft/weo/2015/01/weodata/index.aspx.
[a] Per capita GDP is measured in purchasing power parity.

In South America, Colombia, Ecuador, Chile, Brazil and Peru have the highest implementation rates. Chile, Colombia and Peru have free trade agreements with the United States and the European Union, which include trade facilitation provisions. Ecuador has implemented the ECUAPASS computer system (based on the UNI-PASS system in the Republic of Korea), which has enabled almost all customs procedures to be digitalized. At the other end of the scale, the Plurinational State of Bolivia has an implementation rate well below the subregional average (22 percentage points).

With an average implementation rate of 51%, the Caribbean lags well behind the other two subregions. The Dominican Republic scores best within this group, as it is a CAFTA-DR member country and has therefore had to implement the trade facilitation commitments contained in that agreement. The results for this subregion should be interpreted with caution, as only four countries completed the questionnaire. Nevertheless, it is clear that the challenges faced by the Caribbean are different to those of the rest of the region, including the island status and small size of the subregion's economies, the limited availability of air and sea connections between them and high levels of public debt that restrict the fiscal space to invest in modernizing foreign trade procedures.

2. The region's major achievement has been to increase the transparency of its regulatory frameworks

The results of the questionnaire reveal considerable variations in implementation rates for specific measures (see table III.4).[4] The highest regional average was in the category of transparency (78%), particularly when it came to the region's record on publishing legislation and regulations on the Internet, issuing advance rulings on tariff classification and establishing independent appeals mechanisms for challenging customs rulings. The Central America

---

4   The implementation rates for each category are a simple average of implementation rates for all the measures included in that category.

and Mexico subregion had the highest implementation rate in this category (87%), followed by South America (83%) and, trailing a long way behind, the Caribbean (55%). In all three subregions, the transparency measures with the lowest implementation rates were stakeholder consultation on new draft regulations and advance publication and notification of new regulations prior to their entry into force (see figure III.4).

Table III.4
Latin America and the Caribbean (19 countries): [a] **measures with the highest and lowest implementation rates in the Global Survey on Trade Facilitation and Paperless Trade Implementation 2015**
(Percentages)

Category	Most implemented measures	Percentage	Least implemented measures	Percentage
Transparency	Independent mechanism for appealing customs rulings	91	Stakeholder consultation on new draft regulations	70
	Publication of trade regulations on the Internet	86	Advance publication or notification of new regulations before their implementation	60
Formalities	Post-clearance audit	88	Trade facilitation measures for authorized operators	60
	Provisions for expedited shipments	86	Establishment and publication of average release times	39
Institutional arrangements and cooperation	Cooperation among different national border agencies	74	Establishment of national trade facilitation committees	49
			Other government agencies delegate control to customs authorities	40
Paperless trade	Electronic or automated customs system	98	Electronic single window system for foreign trade	60
	Internet connection available to agencies at border crossings	90	Electronic application for customs refunds	32
Cross-border paperless trade	Electronic transactions legislation	88	Certificates of origin exchanged electronically	28
	Recognized authority for certifying electronic signatures	56	Sanitary and phytosanitary certificates exchanged electronically	11
Transit facilitation	Supporting pre-arrival processing	67	Cooperation between the agencies of countries involved in transit	61
	Physical inspections of goods in transit limited and risk assessments used	65		

Source: Economic Commission for Latin America and the Caribbean (ECLAC), on the basis of information from the Global Survey on Trade Facilitation and Paperless Trade Implementation 2015.
[a] Barbados, Brazil, Chile, Colombia, Costa Rica, Dominican Republic, Ecuador, El Salvador, Guatemala, Honduras, Mexico, Nicaragua, Panama, Paraguay, Peru, Plurinational State of Bolivia, Suriname, Trinidad and Tobago and Uruguay.

Figure III.4
Latin America and the Caribbean (19 countries): [a] **average implementation rates for transparency measures by subregion, 2015**
(Percentages)

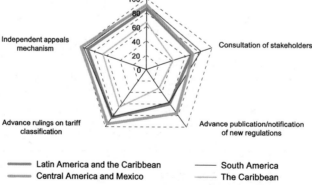

Source: Economic Commission for Latin America and the Caribbean (ECLAC), on the basis of information from the Global Survey on Trade Facilitation and Paperless Trade Implementation 2015.
[a] Barbados, Brazil, Chile, Colombia, Costa Rica, Dominican Republic, Ecuador, El Salvador, Guatemala, Honduras, Mexico, Nicaragua, Panama, Paraguay, Peru, Plurinational State of Bolivia, Suriname, Trinidad and Tobago and Uruguay.

In the category of trade formalities, the regional implementation percentage is above 80% for several measures, namely post-clearance audits, facilities for expedited shipments, risk management and pre-arrival processing. The measures with the lowest implementation rates are facilitation measures for authorized operators and the regular publication of average release times. By subregion, the pattern is similar to that for transparency measures. With few exceptions, the countries of Central America and Mexico and of South America have implemented all the measures in full or at least partially, unlike those of the Caribbean (see figure III.5).

Figure III.5
Latin America and the Caribbean (19 countries): [a] **average implementation rates for formalities-related measures by subregion, 2015**
(Percentages)

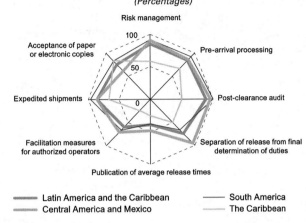

Source: Economic Commission for Latin America and the Caribbean (ECLAC), on the basis of information from the Global Survey on Trade Facilitation and Paperless Trade Implementation 2015.
[a] Barbados, Brazil, Chile, Colombia, Costa Rica, Dominican Republic, Ecuador, El Salvador, Guatemala, Honduras, Mexico, Nicaragua, Panama, Paraguay, Peru, Plurinational State of Bolivia, Suriname, Trinidad and Tobago and Uruguay.

In the category of paperless trade, the implementation rate for several measures is above average, specifically the use of automated customs systems (98%), Internet connection available to customs and other public agencies at border crossings (90%), electronic payment of customs duties and other fees (86%), electronic submission of customs declarations (84%) and electronic submission of air cargo manifests (77%). Measures with a lower implementation rate are electronic single window systems (60%) and, most particularly, the option to apply for refunds of customs payments electronically (32%). By subregion, South America has the highest implementation rate (81%), followed by Central America and Mexico (73%) and the Caribbean (61%) (see figure III.6).

Figure III.6
Latin America and the Caribbean (19 countries): [a] **average implementation rates for paperless trade measures by subregion, 2015**
(Percentages)

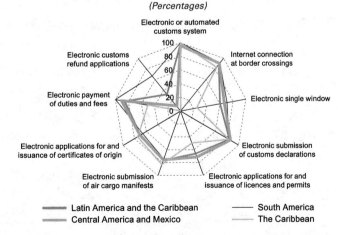

Source: Economic Commission for Latin America and the Caribbean (ECLAC), on the basis of information from the Global Survey on Trade Facilitation and Paperless Trade Implementation 2015.
[a] Barbados, Brazil, Chile, Colombia, Costa Rica, Dominican Republic, Ecuador, El Salvador, Guatemala, Honduras, Mexico, Nicaragua, Panama, Paraguay, Peru, Plurinational State of Bolivia, Suriname, Trinidad and Tobago and Uruguay.

Electronic single window systems are essential for paperless trade as they provide the basis for implementing several of the other measures. The implementation rate for this tool is much higher in South America (71%) and the Central America and Mexico subregion (67%) than in the Caribbean (25%).

All the participating countries in South America except the Plurinational State of Bolivia reported that an electronic single window system had been fully or partially implemented. Implementation remains partial in Brazil, Chile, Paraguay and Uruguay, either because their electronic single windows are currently only available for either export or import operations (but not both), or because they still require hard copies of some documents or the physical presence of interested parties for certain operations. The latter is the case in Brazil, which is currently in the process of digitalizing all procedures. Colombia, Ecuador and Peru now have fully operational electronic single windows. The system in place in Peru, created in 2006, is one of the most advanced in the region, covering import, export and customs transit operations. It owes its success to an adequate legal framework, the participation of more than 12 public agencies and the involvement of the private sector in its creation and development.

All the Central American countries reported that electronic single window systems had been partially implemented, with the exception of Nicaragua, which was still in the pilot phase. The single window system in place in El Salvador is particularly noteworthy. Although it is only fully operational for exports, it allows data to be shared electronically with Guatemala, Honduras and Nicaragua, thanks to a digital infrastructure linking up customs offices and other relevant agencies within the subregion. El Salvador is implementing an electronic single window for imports, which is expected to be operational by the end of 2015. Mexico is the only country in the subregion that has fully implemented an electronic single window for import, export and transit operations.

Of the four participating Caribbean countries, Trinidad and Tobago has made the most progress, with a partially implemented electronic single window. The Dominican Republic is still in the pilot phase, while Barbados and Suriname have not begun implementation. The electronic single window in Trinidad and Tobago, launched in 2009 under the name TTBizLink, has a particularly wide range of functionalities. It can be used not only for foreign trade procedures but also to undertake tasks electronically, such as registering a company or applying for work permits and tax benefits.

The greater complexity of cross-border paperless trade is reflected in the low implementation rates of the region (47%) and its three subregions. This result is not surprising as these measures require not only a sophisticated technological infrastructure, but also close cooperation among the relevant bodies of the countries sharing documentation. Central America's leadership in this area, with an implementation rate of 55%, reflects efforts to expedite trade through electronic document sharing, most notably via the project known as the Meso-American International Transit of Merchandise (TIM), which was launched in 2008 between El Salvador and Honduras and has gradually been extended throughout the subregion.

3. Despite the progress, significant challenges remain

Participating countries identified the main areas or specific trade facilitation measures in which they had made progress in the 12 months prior to the survey. The most frequently mentioned measures were the establishment of authorized operator schemes, the creation or expansion of electronic single windows, and electronic submission or issuance of documentation (see figure III.7). Countries also identified the main problems they faced. Their responses dwelt more on the lack of coordination among the government bodies involved and human resource limitations than on financial constraints and insufficient availability of information and communications technology infrastructure (see figure III.8).

Although trade facilitation is often seen as relevant only to customs authorities, in practice it concerns many other public bodies that perform border inspections or issue documents required for foreign trade transactions, such as ministries of transport, health and environment protection services. However, not all these bodies are mandated or expected to expedite trade flows. There is therefore considerable potential for conflict (for example, when appointing a lead agency to oversee implementation of the trade facilitation agenda) and a pressing need for coordination among public bodies. The current preparatory period leading up to implementation of the TFA is a window of opportunity to identify the most appropriate institutional frameworks for overcoming these challenges.

Figure III.7
Latin America and the Caribbean (19 countries): [a] **trade facilitation measures in which most progress was made in the 12 months prior to the Global Survey on Trade Facilitation and Paperless Trade Implementation 2015**
(Number of mentions)

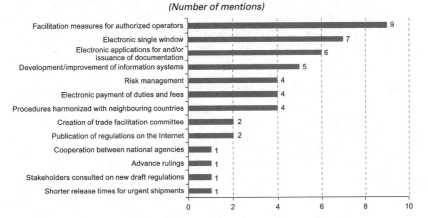

Source: Economic Commission for Latin America and the Caribbean (ECLAC), on the basis of information from the Global Survey on Trade Facilitation and Paperless Trade Implementation 2015.
[a] Barbados, Brazil, Chile, Colombia, Costa Rica, Dominican Republic, Ecuador, El Salvador, Guatemala, Honduras, Mexico, Nicaragua, Panama, Paraguay, Peru, Plurinational State of Bolivia, Suriname, Trinidad and Tobago and Uruguay.

Figure III.8
Latin America and the Caribbean (19 countries): [a] **main challenges faced by each country in implementing trade facilitation measures, 2015**
(Number of mentions)

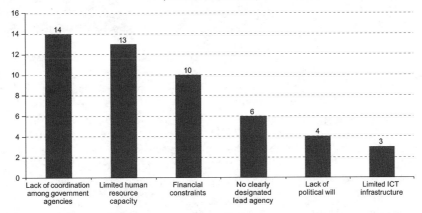

Source: Economic Commission for Latin America and the Caribbean (ECLAC), on the basis of information from the Global Survey on Trade Facilitation and Paperless Trade Implementation 2015.
[a] Barbados, Brazil, Chile, Colombia, Costa Rica, Dominican Republic, Ecuador, El Salvador, Guatemala, Honduras, Mexico, Nicaragua, Panama, Paraguay, Peru, Plurinational State of Bolivia, Suriname, Trinidad and Tobago and Uruguay.

C. Institutional development to facilitate trade and support export diversification

The region needs to make progress on the trade facilitation agenda for a number of reasons. Expediting trade flows between its countries would help to increase the current low levels of intraregional trade. Moreover, since inefficiencies in border procedures disproportionally affect smaller companies (the vast majority of which do not export), trade facilitation may promote their internationalization. This, in turn, may encourage export diversification and reduce the region's, and particularly South America's, current dependence on raw materials.

In the past two decades, the most dynamic and technology-intensive trade flows have largely taken place within regional or global value chains wherein trade facilitation is a factor for competitiveness. If the production of a final good is divided between two or more countries, the number of cross-border transactions increases, in particular for parts, components and other inputs. This, in turn, increases the cost of inefficiencies in document management and administrative procedures at borders. This cost is particularly high in perishable goods chains, those that operate with small inventories and those that must adapt their product specifications quickly to changes in demand (in the apparel industry, for example).[5]

In light of the foregoing, progress in trade facilitation could strengthen weak intraregional production chains and increase the region's presence in global value chains, which is still very limited. Several concepts that underpin the trade facilitation agenda, such as making government agencies more transparent and efficient and promoting public-private dialogue, are also crucial for increasing State efficiency and combating corruption.

Latin America and the Caribbean's progress in implementing the trade facilitation agenda has been considerable, albeit uneven, with South America and Central America and Mexico performing much better than the Caribbean. Through its regional aid for trade strategy, the Caribbean seeks to secure international cooperation resources for a limited number of high-impact initiatives, including several related to trade facilitation.

Some of the measures in which there has been relatively modest progress across the region do not require substantial financial investments. This is the case for the creation of national trade facilitation committees, the regular publication of average times for release of traded goods and the advance publication of new regulations before they enter into force. The main factors constraining implementation of these measures could be of a political or institutional nature such as, for example, trade facilitation not being perceived as a political priority or some agencies being reluctant to submit to higher standards of transparency and accountability.

The cross-cutting nature of the trade facilitation agenda raises serious institutional challenges for the countries of the region. A great deal of thought must therefore be given to the design of national trade facilitation committees in order to secure a commitment from political authorities (should it become necessary to resolve conflicts between agencies, for example) and effective public-private coordination.

One last reflection relates to the role of economic integration agreements. The Global Survey results show that several countries in the region have made considerable progress, but the impact of that progress would be greater if it were coordinated at the regional or at least the subregional level. For example, if the aim is to ease the operations of regional value chains, it would be preferable for a number of countries to agree among themselves on the criteria a firm has to meet to be considered an authorized operator, or on the content of advance rulings. Similarly, the design of the procedures needed to ensure full interoperability of national single windows should be coordinated at the regional or subregional level. The experience of Central America illustrates the benefits of coordinating with neighbouring countries on these matters. The recent discussions undertaken between the Pacific Alliance and the Southern Common Market (MERCOSUR) with a view to exploring the scope for joint trade facilitation work have great potential to boost trade and productive integration throughout the region.

---

[5] Moisé and Sorescu (2015) conclude that there is a positive relationship between trade facilitation measures and the level and strength of participation in value chains. An increase of 0.1 of a point in a country's performance on the OECD trade facilitation indicators (whose scale runs from 0 to 2) could increase its imports of foreign value added by between 1.5% and 3.5% and its exports of local value added by between 1% and 3%.

Bibliography

Duval, Yann, Tengfei Wang and Dimitra Tsoulou Malakoudi (2015), *Trade Facilitation and Paperless Trade Implementation Survey 2015. Asia and the Pacific Report*, Bangkok, Economic and Social Commission for Asia and the Pacific (ESCAP), July [online] http://www.unescap.org/sites/default/files/UNRCsTFPTSurvey_ESCAP_Regional_Report2015_0.pdf.

ECE (Economic Commission for Europe) (2005), "Recommendation and guidelines on establishing a single window to enhance the efficient exchange of information between trade and government", Recommendation, No. 33, New York, July.

García, Tania and Sebastián Herreros (2015), *Trade Facilitation and Paperless Trade Implementation Survey 2015. Latin America and the Caribbean*, Santiago, Economic Commission for Latin America and the Caribbean (ECLAC), August.

IDB (Inter-American Development Bank) (2013), "Too Far to Export: Domestic Transport Costs and Regional Export Disparities in Latin America and the Caribbean", [online] https://publications.iadb.org/handle/11319/3664?locale-attribute=en, Washington.

Jaimurzina, Azhar (2014), "The future of trade and transport facilitation: implications of the WTO Trade Facilitation Agreement", *FAL Bulletin*, No. 333, Santiago, Economic Commission for Latin America and the Caribbean (ECLAC), November.

Lardé, Jeannette and Ricardo J. Sánchez (2014), "The economic infrastructure gap and investment in Latin America", *FAL Bulletin*, No. 332, Economic Commission for Latin America and the Caribbean (ECLAC), October.

Moisé, Evdokia, Thomas Orliac and Peter Minor (2011), "Trade facilitation indicators. The impact on trade costs", *OECD Trade Policy Papers*, No. 118, Paris.

Moisé, Evdokia and Silvia Sorescu (2015), "Contribution of trade facilitation measures to the operation of supply chains", *OECD Trade Policy Papers*, No. 181, Paris.

___ (2013), "Trade facilitation indicators. The potential impact of trade facilitation on developing countries' trade", *OECD Trade Policy Papers*, No. 144, Paris.

Neufeld, Nora (2014), "The long and winding road: how WTO members finally reached a Trade Facilitation Agreement", *Staff Working Paper ERSD*, No. 2014-06, Geneva, April [online] http://wto.org/english/res_e/reser_e/ersd201406_e.pdf.

OECD (Organization for Economic Cooperation and Development) (2015), "Implementation of the WTO Trade Facilitation Agreement: The potential impact on trade costs", Paris, June [online] http://www.oecd.org/tad/tradedev/WTO-TF-Implementation-Policy-Brief_EN_2015_06.pdf.

Perrotti, Daniel and Ricardo J. Sánchez (2011), "La brecha de infraestructura en América Latina y el Caribe", *Recursos Naturales e Infraestructura series*, No. 153 (LC/L.3342), Santiago, Economic Commission for Latin America and the Caribbean (ECLAC).

World Bank (2015), *Doing Business 2015: Going Beyond Efficiency*, Washington D.C. [online] www.doingbusiness.org/reports/global-reports/doing-business-2015.

Annex III.A1

The World Trade Organization Trade Facilitation Agreement

The negotiations on the Trade Facilitation Agreement (TFA) were concluded at the Ninth Ministerial Conference of the World Trade Organization (WTO) (Bali, December 2013). While the General Agreement on Tariffs and Trade (GATT) contains provisions relating to trade facilitation (articles V, VIII and X), those in the TFA are more specific and up-to-date.

Section I of the TFA contains the substantive commitments that WTO members must accept:

Article 1: Publication and availability of information

Article 2: Opportunity to comment, information before entry into force, and consultations

Article 3: Advance rulings

Article 4: Procedures for appeal or review

Article 5: Other measures to enhance impartiality, non-discrimination and transparency

Article 6: Disciplines on fees and charges imposed on or in connection with importation and exportation and penalties

Article 7: Release and clearance of goods

Article 8: Border agency cooperation

Article 9: Movement of goods intended for import under customs control

Article 10: Formalities connected with importation, exportation and transit

Article 11: Freedom of transit

Article 12: Customs cooperation

Section II of the TFA, which addresses special and differential treatment for developing and least-developed country members, indicates that the commitments set out in section I can be implemented based on three categories relating to timeframes and conditions for implementation. The three categories are:

Category A: provisions that each country designates for implementation upon entry into force of the agreement or, in the case of a least-developed country member, within one year after entry into force.

Category B: provisions that each country designates for implementation at a later date as established by the country in question.

Category C: provisions that each country designates for implementation at a later date, decided by the country in question and subject to receiving necessary assistance.

Each developing or least-developed country can decide which provisions to include under each category. This manner in which special and differential treatment is addressed is an innovative approach, both because of its individualized character and because it makes implementation of certain provisions conditional upon countries receiving the necessary assistance. In the same vein, grace periods were established during which developing and least-developed countries cannot be named as respondents in the WTO dispute settlement mechanism in connection with the implementation of their TFA obligations. These periods range from 2 to 8 years after the entry into force of the TFA, depending on whether the country in question is a developing or least-developed country and in which category the respective provision falls.

Section III of the TFA provides for the establishment of a committee on trade facilitation in WTO and national committees on trade facilitation in each of its member States. National committees will have the task of facilitating both domestic coordination and implementation of TFA provisions.

The TFA is in the process of being ratified and will enter into force (in member States that have ratified it) once this has taken place in two thirds of WTO member States (161 as of August 2015). As of the writing of this publication, 50 WTO member States, including three from the region (Belize, Nicaragua and Trinidad and Tobago), have ratified the TFA.

Annex III.A2

Categories of measures on the trade facilitation agenda

The classification adopted by the Economic and Social Commission for Asia and the Pacific (ESCAP) identifies five groups of measures that comprise the trade facilitation agenda (Duval, Wang and Tsoulou Malakoudi, 2015).

1. Transparency

This group includes the online publication of legislation, rulings, circulars and other regulations, consultations with the private sector on new draft regulations, the advance publication of these before their implementation, the issuance of advance rulings and the establishment of appeal or review procedures (articles 1 to 4 of the TFA).

An advance ruling is a binding written decision issued by the customs agency of an importing country at the request of an interested party (usually an importer or exporter) prior to the arrival of the merchandise covered by the application. The ruling sets forth the treatment the merchandise will be given upon arrival in the country with respect to, at least, its tariff classification and origin. Other aspects that might be included are the method to be used to determine the customs value of the merchandise and the applicable tariff treatment. The TFA indicates that WTO member States shall, at a minimum, publish the requirements for an advance ruling application, the time it will take to issue the ruling, and the length of time for which it will remain valid. It also states that WTO members shall guarantee the right of anyone affected by an administrative customs decision to seek review and, where applicable, rectification by a higher administrative authority, a judicial body, or both.

2. Formalities

This group includes mainly measures contained in article 7 of the TFA and covers nine topics:

- Pre-arrival processing. This allows for import documentation and other information required for the release of imported goods to be submitted before they arrive, to expedite their release.
- Risk management. This refers to methods or practices customs authorities use to determine which transactions or which importers, exporters or transit operators shall be subject to checks, such as physical inspections, and the type and extent of checks to be applied. The TFA encourages countries to concentrate customs checks on high-risk consignments and to expedite the release of low-risk consignments by using appropriate selection criteria.
- Separation of release from final determination of customs duties, taxes, fees and charges. This allows goods to be released prior to the final determination of these payments, provided that all other regulatory requirements have been met. The customs authorities of the importing country may require a guarantee in the form of a surety, deposit or other instrument.
- Post-clearance audit. In order to expedite the release of goods, the authorities shall verify compliance with customs and related laws and regulations by inspecting traders' ledgers and post-clearance registries.
- Establishment and publication of average release times. This encourages customs authorities to periodically calculate and publish information on these times.
- Authorized operators. This entails benefits for companies known as authorized operators. The advantages offered may include, among other things, fewer documentation or physical inspection requirements and deferred payment of customs duties, taxes, fees and charges. The criteria for qualifying as an authorized operator include a good record of compliance with customs laws and regulations, financial solvency and supply chain security.
- Urgent shipments. The aim is to speed up processing of documents and goods imported by operators of urgent delivery services.
- Perishable goods. The aim is to expedite clearance of such goods, for example, by prioritizing them when inspections are scheduled.
- Acceptance of copies. Customs and other bodies may accept paper or electronic copies of the documents required for import, export or transit formalities.

3. Institutional arrangements and cooperation

This includes the creation of national committees on trade facilitation and national or international cooperation between the bodies responsible for border controls and procedures relating to the import, export and transit of goods (articles 8, 12 and 23 of the TFA). An example of national cooperation is coordination between customs and health protection services to carry out simultaneous physical inspections of shipments. Examples of international cooperation include the exchange of information between customs authorities and coordination between countries that share common borders to align their procedures and formalities or the working days and hours of their border posts.

4. Paperless trade

This seeks to facilitate the flow of documentation using information and communications technologies (articles 7 and 10 of the TFA). It includes measures such as the use of electronic single windows for foreign trade, electronic payment of duties or other related charges, and applications, issuance and sharing of documents across borders (customs declarations, sanitary and phytosanitary certificates, import licences, environmental authorizations and certificates of origin).

Paperless trade has both an internal and a cross-border dimension. Internal measures include streamlining the procedures required of operators by national authorities, such as paying duties or obtaining documents. The cross-border dimension is the option for traders and authorities in two or more countries involved in a trade transaction to share documents electronically.

The basis for paperless trade is a single window for foreign trade. This is defined as "a facility that allows parties involved in trade and transport to lodge standardized information and documents with a single entry point to fulfil all import, export and transit-related regulatory requirements. If information is electronic, then individual data elements should only be submitted once" (ECE, 2005). Establishing a single window for foreign trade reduces the time and costs associated with customs formalities and allows the relevant public bodies to manage these formalities in a more efficient, coordinated and transparent manner.

5. Transit facilitation

This includes measures to expedite the movement of goods transiting through one country on the way to their final destination in another (article 11 of the TFA), such as physically separate infrastructure (for example, separate berths) for traffic in transit, pre-arrival submission and processing of transit documents and data and the exemption of goods in transit from technical regulations.

Publicaciones recientes de la CEPAL
ECLAC recent publications

www.cepal.org/publicaciones

Informes periódicos / *Annual reports*
También disponibles para años anteriores / *Issues for previous years also available*

- Estudio Económico de América Latina y el Caribe 2015, 204 p.
  Economic Survey of Latin America and the Caribbean 2015, 196 p.
- La Inversión Extranjera Directa en América Latina y el Caribe 2015, 150 p.
  Foreign Direct Investment in Latin America and the Caribbean 2015, 140 p.
- Anuario Estadístico de América Latina y el Caribe 2014 / *Statistical Yearbook for Latin America and the Caribbean 2014, 238 p.*
- Balance Preliminar de las Economías de América Latina y el Caribe 2014, 92 p.
  Preliminary Overview of the Economies of Latin America and the Caribbean 2014, 92 p.
- Panorama Social de América Latina 2014, 296 p.
  Social Panorama of Latin America 2014, 284 p.
- Panorama de la Inserción Internacional de América Latina y el Caribe 2014, 148 p.
  Latin America and the Caribbean in the World Economy 2014, 140 p.

Libros y documentos institucionales / *Institutional books and documents*

- La nueva revolución digital: de la Internet del consumo a la Internet de la producción, 2015, 98 p.
  The new digital revolution: From the consumer Internet to the industrial Internet, 2015, 98 p.
- Panorama fiscal de América Latina y el Caribe 2015: dilemas y espacios de políticas, 2015, 128 p.
  Fiscal Panorama of Latin America and the Caribbean 2015: Policy space and dilemmas. Executive Summary, 2015, 14 p.
- La economía del cambio climático en América Latina y el Caribe: paradojas y desafíos del desarrollo sostenible, 2014, 96 p.
  The economics of climate change in Latin America and the Caribbean: Paradoxes and challenges of sustainable development, 2014, 92 p.
- El desafío de la sostenibilidad ambiental en América Latina y el Caribe: textos seleccionados de la CEPAL 2012-2014, 2015, 148 p.
- Los pueblos indígenas en América Latina: avances en el último decenio y retos pendientes para la garantía de sus derechos, 2014, 410 p.
- Pactos para la igualdad: hacia un futuro sostenible, 2014, 340 p.
  Covenants for Equality: Towards a sustainable future, 2014, 330 p.
- Integración regional: hacia una estrategia de cadenas de valor inclusivas, 2014, 226 p.
  Regional Integration: Towards an inclusive value chain strategy, 2014, 218 p.
  Integração regional: por uma estratégia de cadeias de valor inclusivas, 2014, 226 p.
- Reflexiones sobre el desarrollo en América Latina y el Caribe. Conferencias magistrales 2013-2014, 2014, 100 p.
- Prospectiva y desarrollo: el clima de la igualdad en América Latina y el Caribe a 2020, 2013, 72 p.
- Comercio internacional y desarrollo inclusivo: construyendo sinergias, 2013, 210 p.
  International trade and inclusive development: Building synergies, 2013, 200 p.
- Cambio estructural para la igualdad: una visión integrada del desarrollo, 2012, 330 p.
  Structural Change for Equality: An integrated approach to development, 2012, 308 p.
- La hora de la igualdad: brechas por cerrar, caminos por abrir, 2010, 290 p.
  Time for Equality: Closing gaps, opening trails, 2010, 270 p.
  A Hora da Igualdade: Brechas por fechar, caminhos por abrir, 2010, 268 p.

Libros de la CEPAL / *ECLAC books*

136 Instrumentos de protección social: caminos latinoamericanos hacia la universalización, Simone Cecchini, Fernando Filgueira, Rodrigo Martínez, Cecilia Rossel (eds.), 2015, 510 p.

135 *Rising concentration in Asia-Latin American value chains: Can small firms turn the tide?* Osvaldo Rosales, Osvaldo, Keiji Inoue, Nanno Mulder (eds.), 2015, 282 p.

134 Desigualdad, concentración del ingreso y tributación sobre las altas rentas en América Latina, Juan Pablo Jiménez (ed.), 2015, 172 p.

133 Desigualdad e informalidad: un análisis de cinco experiencias latinoamericanas, Verónica Amarante, Rodrigo Arim (eds.), 2015, 526 p.

132 Neoestructuralismo y corrientes heterodoxas en América Latina y el Caribe a inicios del siglo XXI, Alicia Bárcena, Antonio Prado (eds.), 2014, 452 p.

131 El nuevo paradigma productivo y tecnólogico: la necesidad de políticas para la autonomía económica de las mujeres, Lucía Scuro, Néstor Bercovich (eds.), 2014, 188 p.

130 Políticas públicas para la igualdad de género: un aporte a la autonomía de las mujeres, María Cristina Benavente, Alejandra Valdés, 2014, 134 p.

129 Prospectiva y política pública para el cambio estructural en América Latina y el Caribe, Javier Medina Vásquez, Steven Becerra y Paola Castaño, 2014, 338 p.

128 Inestabilidad y desigualdad: la vulnerabilidad del crecimiento en América Latina y el Caribe, Juan Alberto Fuentes Knight (ed.), 2014, 304 p.

Copublicaciones / *Co-publications*

- Gobernanza global y desarrollo: nuevos desafíos y prioridades de la cooperación internacional, José Antonio Ocampo (ed.), CEPAL/Siglo Veintiuno, Argentina, 2015, 286 p.

- *Decentralization and Reform in Latin America: Improving Intergovernmental Relations, Giorgio Brosio and Juan Pablo Jiménez (eds.), ECLAC / Edward Elgar Publishing, United Kingdom, 2012, 450 p.*

- Sentido de pertenencia en sociedades fragmentadas: América Latina desde una perspectiva global, Martín Hopenhayn y Ana Sojo (comps.), CEPAL / Siglo Veintiuno, Argentina, 2011, 350 p.

Coediciones / *Co-editions*

- Perspectivas económicas de América Latina 2015: educación, competencias e innovación para el desarrollo, CEPAL/OCDE, 2014, 200 p.
  Latin American Economic Outlook 2015: Education, skills and innovation for development, ECLAC,/CAF/OECD, 2014, 188 p.

- *Regional Perspectives on Sustainable Development: Advancing Integration of its Three Dimensions through Regional Action, ECLAC-ECE-ESCAP-ESCWA, 2014, 114 p.*

- Perspectivas de la agricultura y del desarrollo rural en las Américas: una mirada hacia América Latina y el Caribe 2014, CEPAL / FAO / IICA, 2013, 220 p.

Cuadernos de la CEPAL

101 Redistribuir el cuidado: el desafío de las políticas, Coral Calderón Magaña (coord.), 2013, 460 p.

101 *Redistributing care: The policy challenge, Coral Calderón Magaña (coord.), 2013, 420 p.*

100 Construyendo autonomía: compromiso e indicadores de género, Karina Batthyáni Dighiero, 2012, 338 p.

Documentos de proyecto / *Project documents*

- La economía del cambio climático en el Perú, 2014, 152 p.

- La economía del cambio climático en la Argentina: primera aproximación, 2014, 240 p.

- La economía del cambio climático en el Ecuador 2012, 2012, 206 p.

Cuadernos estadísticos de la CEPAL

42 Resultados del Programa de Comparación Internacional (PCI) de 2011 para América Latina y el Caribe. Solo disponible en CD, 2015.

41 Los cuadros de oferta y utilización, las matrices de insumo-producto y las matrices de empleo. Solo disponible en CD, 2013.

Series de la CEPAL / *ECLAC Series*

Asuntos de Género / Comercio Internacional / Desarrollo Productivo / Desarrollo Territorial / Estudios Estadísticos / Estudios y Perspectivas (Bogotá, Brasilia, Buenos Aires, México, Montevideo) / *Studies and Perspectives* (The Caribbean, Washington) / Financiamiento del Desarrollo/ Gestión Pública / Informes y Estudios Especiales / Macroeconomía del Desarrollo / Manuales / Medio Ambiente y Desarrollo / Población y Desarrollo/ Política Fiscal / Políticas Sociales / Recursos Naturales e Infraestructura / Seminarios y Conferencias.

Revista CEPAL / *CEPAL Review*

La Revista se inició en 1976, con el propósito de contribuir al examen de los problemas del desarrollo socioeconómico de la región. La *Revista CEPAL* se publica en español e inglés tres veces por año.

CEPAL Review first appeared in 1976, its aim being to make a contribution to the study of the economic and social development problems of the region. CEPAL Review is published in Spanish and English versions three times a year.

Observatorio demográfico / *Demographic Observatory*

Edición bilingüe (español e inglés) que proporciona información estadística actualizada, referente a estimaciones y proyecciones de población de los países de América Latina y el Caribe. Desde 2013 el Observatorio aparece una vez al año.

Bilingual publication (Spanish and English) proving up-to-date estimates and projections of the populations of the Latin American and Caribbean countries. Since 2013, the Observatory appears once a year.

Notas de población

Revista especializada que publica artículos e informes acerca de las investigaciones más recientes sobre la dinámica demográfica en la región. También incluye información sobre actividades científicas y profesionales en el campo de población.
La revista se publica desde 1973 y aparece dos veces al año, en junio y diciembre.

Specialized journal which publishes articles and reports on recent studies of demographic dynamics in the region. Also includes information on scientific and professional activities in the field of population.
Published since 1973, the journal appears twice a year in June and December.

Las publicaciones de la CEPAL están disponibles en:
ECLAC publications are available at:

www.cepal.org/publicaciones

También se pueden adquirir a través de:
They can also be ordered through:

www.un.org/publications

United Nations Publications
PO Box 960
Herndon, VA 20172
USA

Tel. (1-888)254-4286
Fax (1-800)338-4550
Contacto / *Contact*: publications@un.org
Pedidos / *Orders*: order@un.org